D0605661

MANGIAMO

The Sebastiani Family Cookbook

BY SYLVIA SEBASTIANI

PUBLISHED BY SILVERBACK BOOKS, INC.

In memory of Sylvia Sebastiani

Sylvia and August Sebastiani at their home in Sonoma, circa 1965

Copyright © 1970, 2005 by Sebastiani Vineyards & Winery
All rights reserved.
No part of this book may be reproduced in any form whatsoever except by a newspaper or magazine reviewer who wishes to quote brief
passages in connection with a review.

Printed in China

Library of Congress Cataloging in Publication Data
Sebastiani, Sylvia.
The Sebastiani family cookbook.
Published in 1970 under title: *Mangiamo (let's eat!)*
1. Cooking, Italian. I. Title.
TX 723.s37 1977 641.5'945   76-30276

A special thanks to Kelly Conrad and Rose Scarafoni Millerick for their editorial assistance,
and to Jadyne Jeung Buchholz for her tremendous help to my mother editing and typing the first edition.

Project Editor: Lisa Tooker
Art Direction and Design: Kate Berg
Photography: Lisa Keenan Photography*
Food Stylist: Pouke Halpern*
Assistant Food Stylist: Jeff Larsen*
Prop Stylist: Carol Hacker, Tableprop*

*Photography: Cover, pages 2, 9, 14, 16 (top right), 23, 26, 27, 33, 42, 43, 51, 54, 55, 71, 74, 75, 86, 92, 93, 112, 113, 123, 138, 139, 142,
148, 149, 154, 160, 161, 170, 180, 181, 186, 190, 191, 208, 246, 247, 259, 267
Photography: M.J. Wickham: 22, 24

Silverback Books, Inc.
55 New Montgomery Street, #503
San Francisco, CA 94105

www.silverbackbooks.com

CONTENTS

foreword

MY MOTHER, SYLVIA SEBASTIANI, passed away in November of 2003, and her family and friends lost a family matriarch, a devoted friend and the most valuable winery hostess. Cooking for her family and friends was a part of my mother's nature and a way of expressing her love for them.

Sylvia was born in Cordelia (Thomasson), California on May 10th, 1916. Her parents, Guiseppe and Pierina Scarafoni, moved Sylvia and her younger sisters Rose and Violet ("Dolly") to Sonoma in 1927, where they expanded their dairy farm. In 1936, Sylvia married my father, August Sebastiani, and became his partner in Sebastiani Vineyards & Winery. After her father's death in the early 1970s, Sylvia and August planted grapes on her family's dairy in the Carneros region. These vineyards today are known as our Nebbione and Green Acres Vineyards.

Sylvia contributed greatly to the growth and quality of the Sebastiani family winery. Ever the consummate cook, she could entertain a group of up to 30 for lunch with only 20 minutes notice. My mother learned to cook, not only from her mother, but also from her mother-in-law, Elvira Eraldi Sebastiani. My grandmothers' cooking styles were distinctly different, from two separate regions of Italy: Lombardi and Tuscany. My mother's freezer was packed with many Italian dishes. She was always ready for a call from her August to entertain distributors, customers, brokers, and sales people in our family's hilltop home, overlooking the winery and the city of Sonoma. Before the winery had a tasting room and a Hospitality Department, Sylvia hosted all the winery's guests, entertaining them at her home or at the winery amidst the redwood aging casks. In the 1960s, my mother compiled, at her family and friends' urgings, her famous Sebastiani family cookbook *Mangiamo*, meaning "Let's Eat." Over half a million copies are presently in circulation.

When the winery established its tasting room and Hospitality Department, my mother conducted many cooking demonstrations for winery guests. She

Sylvia Sebastiani in the kitchen of her hillside Sonoma home, Casa de Sonoma. (1980s).

appeared regularly on television and in department stores promoting her cookbook. When Sylvia was not in the tasting room signing her cookbook and greeting visitors, she could be found in the winery garden, pruning roses, and giving advice to our winery gardeners. Sylvia loved her award-winning garden and shared her flowers with everyone. Her Bird of Paradise and her Calla Lilies graced her tables of epicurean delight.

As a tribute to the memory of my mother and in honor of Sebastiani Vineyards & Winery's 100-year anniversary, our family wanted to update her cookbook, adding an historical overview, while retaining the classic family recipes. Our family—grandparents, parents, children, grandchildren, great-grandchildren, and our Sebastiani winery family—owes a great deal to my mother's culinary endeavors. The glue that held the family and the winery together was Sylvia's meals around the family dining table.

Keep in mind, this is a collection of old family recipes, some go back 50, 60, and even 100 years. You will find what some might call "dated" recipes in these pages, but I prefer to refer to them as "nostalgic." I could not part with the Gelatin Ribbon Salad recipe, even though I know Jello is an anachronism to some. My father was an avid hunter and fisherman, and consequently, my mother was inspired to prepare his bounty in a mouth-watering fashion. You will find some rather uncommon recipes for wild game, venison heart, and the like, but this book is not without its comfort foods. My mother made homemade soup for my father every day, and there is still nothing like a steaming bowl of Minestrone Soup after a wet, cold day in the vineyards or mushroom hunting in the oak and Madrone-covered hills surrounding Sonoma.

I hope this revised edition of my mother's cookbook allows my mother's culinary spirit to endure through your enjoyment of the recipes within its covers. I wish you and your family many warm and traditional dining experiences.

Mangiamo!

Mary Ann Sebastiani Cuneo

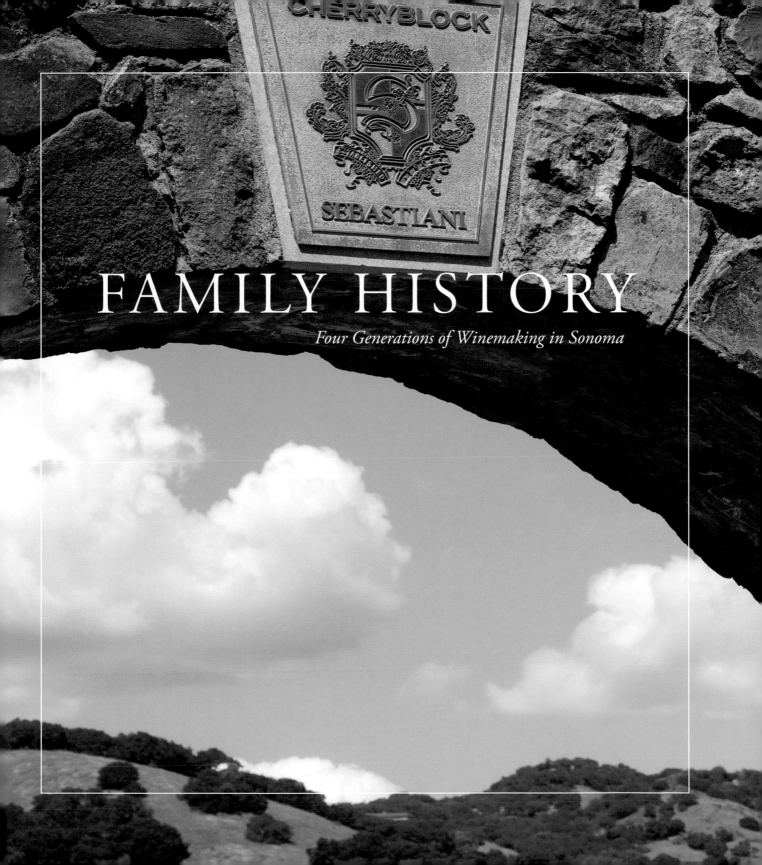

FAMILY HISTORY

Four Generations of Winemaking in Sonoma

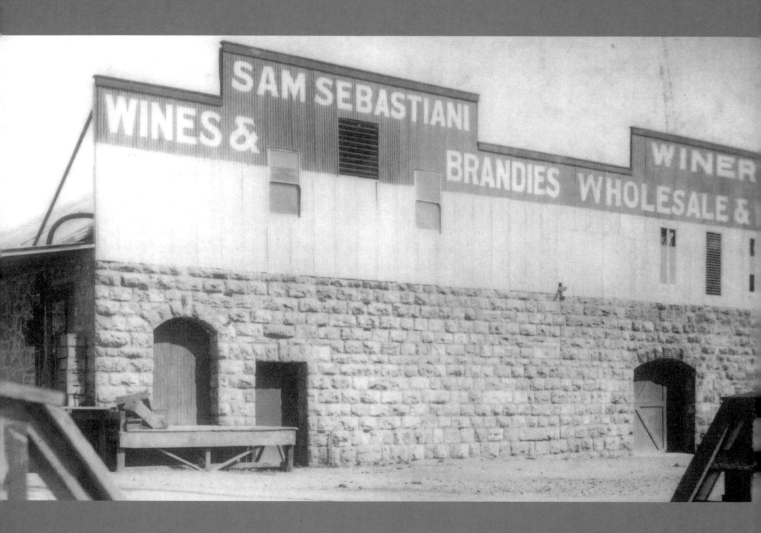

Above: Sebastiani Winery, 1915.

SEBASTIANI VINEYARDS & WINERY is in its second century of family ownership. Samuele (sam-well-eh) Sebastiani founded this winery in 1904. With over 100 years of winemaking experience, Sebastiani has a rich history. The winery estate contains part of the original 1825 Mission Vineyard, where the Northern California wine industry began. Planted by the Franciscan Padres, this vineyard provided sacramental wines for the Mission San Francisco De Solano. This state historical landmark, Number 739, was the first vineyard planted north of San Francisco. Once owned by General Mariano Vallejo, it was later purchased by Samuele Sebastiani. In 1825, only one grape variety was planted in this vineyard, the "Mission Black Grape." Today, two acres of this historic vineyard are located at the winery and are planted to Merlot and Malbec. Grapes from this vineyard are used in Sebastiani's Proprietary Blend Secolo.

The Sebastiani Family, circa 1915.
From left: Sabina Sebastiani
McTaggart, Elvira Eraldi Sebastiani,
August David Sebastiani, Lorenzo
Sebastiani, and Samuele Sebastiani.

Samuele Sebastiani was born in 1874 in the small village of Farneta (Tuscany), Italy. As a young boy, he learned the art of winemaking from the monks of a nearby monastery in Lucca. In 1895 at the age of 21, Samuele immigrated to America with the dream of a better life and a vision of starting his own winery. When he first arrived in America, like most young immigrants of the time, he was very poor. He worked in New York City's Mamma Leone's restaurant until he had earned enough money to take a train to California. Once in California, he worked in the artichoke fields near Colma where he earned enough money for a wagon and a team of horses. He then headed north and settled in Sonoma where he began working at the Sorini Winery for $1.25 per day. He also worked hauling cobblestones from quarries in the Mayacamas Mountains north of Sonoma to pave the streets of San Francisco. At this time, he began making homemade wine and selling it for a nickel a cup to the men working in the quarry. He would ladle it out of a small cask, which he had on the back of his horse-drawn wagon.

MANGIAMO The Sebastiani Family Cookbook

Top: Toiling in the quarry in 1896. Middle: The Star Saloon. Bottom: The Cannery.

Once established in Sonoma, Samuele contacted an uncle, Fioremonte Milani. Milani, as luck would have it, was a local winemaker. In fact, Milani built the original stone winery building in 1903 as a livery stable. The name, F. Milani 1903, is visible on the arch of one of the original stone walls in the Sebastiani Hospitality Center. (The winery's 17-inch thick rock walls provide a cool, humid climate, similar to the wine caves of Europe and ideal for aging fine wines.)

During his first years in Sonoma, Samuele frequented a local saloon called the Star Saloon. Mr. Eraldi, the saloonkeeper, had a pretty, young daughter named Elvira (ell-vee-rah), who Samuele had admired for some time. He and Elvira were wed in 1904, and by all accounts, it was a perfect match. Sam and Elvira later had three children, a daughter named Sabina and two sons, Lorenzo and August.

By 1904, Samuele—with seven years of hard work in the quarries behind him—was able to purchase the winery from his uncle. The transaction occurred with a simple handshake. Samuele made no initial payment. He would travel the country by rail, selling his wine in far off places. Milani allowed Samuele to pay him as the wine was sold.

Samuele instinctively recognized the merits of Sonoma County's climate and rich red clay soils, ideal for growing wine grapes, similar to the soils of his homeland. With 60 acres of vineyards, Samuele made his first wine, Zinfandel, in a 500-gallon redwood tank using a hand crusher, hand press, and hand pump. Samuele's original equipment is on display today in the Sebastiani Hospitality Center. Samuele sold the wine door-to-door from a horse-drawn wagon, filling his neighbors' wine jugs from small wooden barrels. Locals also brought their own jugs to the winery for weekly refills. Within five years, Samuele owned the winery outright. He was shipping wine in bulk to the east coast by rail tank car. He added additional cellars in 1913, ultimately increasing the winery's capacity to the equivalent of 125,000 cases.

Samuele Sebastiani wrote a sonnet in honor of the celebration of his return to Farneta in 1938 (after 42 years in America). The sonnet expressed his gratitude for his success in America. It was printed on silk and is pictured on right. Below: A Sebastiani Decanter, circa 1930.

FESTE SOLENNI A FARNETA
LUGLIO 30-31 - 1 AGOSTO 1938-XVI

CON ANIMO GRATO E RICONOSCENTE

IL SIGNOR SAMUELE SEBASTIANI

RITORNATO DOPO 42 ANNI DALL' AMERICA
AL PAESE NATIVO DI FARNETA
FACENDO CELEBRARE A SUE SPESE
CON DEVOTA SOLENNITÀ

LA FESTA DEL SS.mo CROCIFISSO

IN RINGRAZIAMENTO DEI BENEFICI RICEVUTI
OFFRE IL SEGUENTE

SONETTO

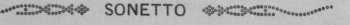

Ecco ritorno dopo il lungo errare
di là dall' Ocean, ecco ritorno,
o dolce Crocifisso, a ringraziare
la tua bontà come promisi un giorno,

Quando varcai, com' esule mendico,
l' umile soglia del paterno foco
e i poggi abbandonai di quest' aprico
silente paesel, con pianto roco.

La tua visione, o veneranda imago,
nell' ore tristi fu la mia difesa
per tua mercè non mi smarrii lontano.

O dolce Crocifisso, il cor è pago
di qui prostrarsi e sciorre in quest' attesa
ora quel voto che non feci invano.

Top: Cuneo Apartments, built by Samuele, 1935. Middle: Sebastiani Theatre (1936) is still located on the Sonoma Square. Bottom: Destruction of wine barrels during Prohibition, 1920.

Samuele felt a strong obligation to the people of Sonoma Valley. In 1918, he built a cannery (which is now the site of the Hospitality Center parking lot) in an effort to provide his workers with jobs during the dormant seasons. The cannery employees canned local meats and tomatoes, as well as other fruits and vegetables. Samuele believed in hard work and managed to keep the cannery and the winery open during Prohibition and the Depression that followed.

Prohibition came as a rude intrusion in 1919 and remained an unwelcome guest until 1933. However, Samuele was able to keep the winery in operation by obtaining one of only ten licenses issued by the government to make altar and medicinal wines. Samuele obtained this license due to his religious devotion: he was a very religious man and contributed generously to the Catholic Church and his local community. The limited production allowed by the license was a small concession; Sam took a financial beating through Prohibition and the Depression. Still, with his strong faith and perseverance, he retained his faithful crew throughout those times and never missed a single payroll.

Samuele felt a deep commitment to give back to the community that provided the foundation of his winemaking dreams. He was an energetic man and along with winemaking, he loved to build things. Construction became a passion. He installed streetlights around town, and he built homes for his employees—he was responsible for many of the homes surrounding the winery on Fourth Street East and Spain Street. After building the homes, Samuele petitioned the city to pave the streets. When the city refused, he paved one side of Fourth Street East at his own expense forcing the city to pave the other half! Samuele made major contributions to the town of Sonoma. He built the Sebastiani Motel, the Sebastiani Hotel, the Sebastiani Apartments, the Sebastiani theatre, the Sebastiani Rollertorium (roller rink), and a Bowling Alley. He also built the first bus depot, a laundromat, a convent, and rebuilt the Catholic Church after it was destroyed by a fire.

Left: Samuele Sebastiani pictured in his 3-piece suite. Lower left: Mary Ann Sebastiani Cuneo with Grandmother Elvira Eraldi Sebastiani, 1950. Above: Sebastiani Family home on 4th Street East, built by Samuele.

Early in his career when Samuele became successful, he dressed according to his stature in life. He wore a three-piece suit and a starched white shirt everyday. This was an Italian trait that Samuele carried on the rest of his life. His daughter-in-law Sylvia said, "He gardened every day, always in his suit. When he harvested his vegetables, he would drive around town giving them to his neighbors and friends. Every Saturday Samuele picked flowers and delivered them to the church for Sunday Mass. He was very generous, always thinking of other people." Samuele Sebastiani passed away in March of 1944 at the age of 70.

TIANI AT REST

COMMUNITY BUILDER

Wine Man, Civic Leader

SYLVIA SEBASTIANI was honored last Saturday as the Valley of the Moon Boys and Girls Club 2000 Sweetheart.

The official opening will be on Sunday, Feb. 26, and the club will be "open for business" starting Monday, Feb. 28.

submitted photo

...due Mrs. Joan ...taff

..., chairman of ...stants, and Ed. Grav... ...r, for the smoothne... ...ency in which the ... ...complished.

The people of the ... ...y are to be than... ...nerosity in contr... ...ward this worth... ...anitarian organ...

The drive wil... ...riday, March ... ...m. so if you ... ...ease phone t...

Celeb

August Sebastiani, Sonoma winemaker, holds two old sea Brant goose decoys used by him hunting on Tomales Bay. His renowned decoy collection will be displayed at the San Francisco Sports and Boat Show which will run from Jan. 11 to 20 at the Cow Palace.

She has a way with food, wine

By ANN ANDERSEN

Forty-five years of mar... ...age to a Sonoma winemaker gave Sylv... Sebastiani an expertis... wine to match her skil... the kitchen. Her cook... "Mangiamo! Let's ... is a collection of her ... ...ly recipes.

She is the wife ... August Sebas... highly regarded ... winemaker wh... over Sebastian... from 1944 unti... 1980. Preside... ...ily-owned w... her son, S... grandfathe...

SYLVIA SEBASTIANI

...helped mark the end of this

age going

...and people in the wine trade. New releases will be offered to restaurateurs and distributors.

Benefit tastings sponsored by local charities will also be held to ...

...an norm... ...clu...apes ripened n... the ...armer days that follo... the summer to produce a b... crop.

on Little Old Winemaker

By GARRY NIVER

...nnie ...ndent ...OM... ...S to

The most beautiful time of the day in Sonoma County's serene Valley of the Moon arrives just before dawn.

And with it, August Sebastiani rises to begin his ... as one of the re... ...rinal litt...

neighbors have yielded to the monetary pressures submitted by the big corporation.

"Just the ... the ...

August Sebastiani conducting his daily wine sampling.

SHORTLY AFTER SAMUELE'S DEATH, HIS SON, AUGUST, AND AUGUST'S WIFE, SYLVIA, PURCHASED THE WINERY FROM SAMUELE'S ESTATE. When they took the winery reigns, most of the wine was sold in bulk. Then one day Sylvia came home raving about a wine she had enjoyed at a Bridge Party. As it turned out, it was a Sebastiani wine under another label. This was an affront to August's ego, and shortly thereafter, August began bottling Sebastiani wine under the Sebastiani Vineyards label.

In the early 1950s, when few wineries were open to the public, Sylvia and August opened the winery doors to visitors for complimentary tastings and tours. The winery became an extension of Sylvia's home and hospitality.

August inherited his father's winemaking talents along with an ability to select the most appropriate sites for specific grape varietals. In 1962, August planted 11 acres of Cabernet Sauvignon on the site of an old cherry orchard, which is now the home of Sebastiani's renowned Cherryblock Vineyard. August's wines became so well regarded that they were served at the 1973 Nixon/Agnew Inaugural Ball at the John F. Kennedy Center.

August soon gained a reputation as one of America's most skilled and innovative winemakers and is still recognized as such to this day. Some of his most notable achievements were in the making and marketing of wine. Before it was customary, August began vintage dating wines. When consumers desired vintage-dated wines, he was prepared. Sebastiani wine became a household word and a legend in the wine industry. In the early 1970s, wine bottle prices escalated and there was a surplus of quality varietal grapes. August used this as an opportunity to introduce varietal wines in reasonably-priced half-gallon bottles. There was overwhelming favorable consumer response, and Sebastiani became the largest varietal wine producer in the United States.

MANGIAMO The Sebastiani Family Cookbook

August Sebastiani in the family's Carneros Vineyard.

August also adapted foreign winemaking concepts to the unique Sonoma climate. He made an Amore Cream Sherry, using the Spanish Solera method. This method involves blending young wines systematically with older wines to maintain a consistent quality and to increase depth of character. August stacked the barrels in the parking lot so the warm Sonoma sun would caramelize the sugars in the exposed upper level barrels. This made the Sebastiani parking lot quite an attraction for visitors. He also introduced Nouveau Beaujolais to Sonoma in the early 1970s. The new-release tasting of Nouveau Gamay Beaujolais is an age-old French custom celebrating the new vintage. Each year on November 15th (approximately three weeks after the harvest), the town of Sonoma bustled with excitement. A trumpet-blaring parade departed from the Mission and traversed

Top: August and Sylvia's home, Casa de Sonoma (completed in 1947), which overlooks the City of Sonoma.

Bottom: August Sebastiani with his beloved swans in his bird sanctuary.

to the winery with casks of August's new release of Gamay Beaujolais. Once at the winery, everyone was invited to sample the new wine over a vintner's lunch. August's celebration caused a media frenzy and became a very famous and popular tradition for many years.

Marvin R. Shanken, Editor and Publisher of the Wine Spectator magazine, wrote in the June 2001 issue that August was a paradox, "a crusty, tire-kicking farmer and, at the same time, a marketing genius. August believed that Sonoma possessed the unique soil and climate conditions necessary to produce great wine." August became a leader and innovator in the industry, and his wines achieved international acclaim.

August was a man of many interests. He enjoyed hunting, fishing, and collecting hand-carved duck decoys. He created a museum of Native American artifacts, a large portion of which now reside at the Santa Rosa Junior College. He also raised horses, cattle and sheep sporadically throughout his life. August was also a noted ornithologist; he took great pride in his bird sanctuary, located at Green Acres Ranch where he spent a lot of time observing and feeding migrating waterfowl. Surrounding his hilltop home were well over 2000 birds in aviaries. August's interest in birds began with waterfowl; his favorite bird was the Pintail Duck. Therefore, there are many duck woodcarvings around the winery facility, as well as a stained glass window depicting August with a swan. August worked with leading scientists and conservationists to preserve the population of the endangered Grayson Dove (Socorro Dove) and to track down the breeding grounds of the Tule Goose.

Top left: Joe Cuneo and Donny Sebastiani at Christmas Dinner, 1988.

Middle left: Sylvia's mother, Pierina Mostachetti Scarafoni.

Right: August Sebastiani pictured front. Back row from left: Richard Cuneo, Don Sebastiani, and Sam Sebastiani, 1974.

August Sebastiani died in February of 1980 at the age of 66. After his death, Sylvia became more actively involved in the winery, both as a Board member and in directing the Hospitality Department. In the '80s and '90s August's sons, Sam and Don Sebastiani, each had a turn at running the winery. During their tenure, the winery grew to 8 million cases. In 1986, Sebastiani became the largest premium winery in California. In 2000, the family decided to sell off all of the (popularly priced) non-Sebastiani brands. Sebastiani returned to its roots and became a single brand winery producing wine exclusively from Sonoma County.

Richard A. Cuneo and Mary Ann
Sebastiani Cuneo with Rubee, their
Boston Terrier.

IN 2001, MARY ANN SEBASTIANI CUNEO
(AUGUST'S ONLY DAUGHTER) BECAME
PRESIDENT AND CEO OF SEBASTIANI
VINEYARDS & WINERY. Mary Ann was raised
with the winery in her front yard. Growing up, she
spent many weekends, summers, and vacations working
on the bottling line, giving tours, and assisting at hospitality events. She earned a bachelor's degree from the
University of Santa Clara in 1969 and a degree in
education from UC Davis in 1970. In 1980, she accepted
a position in marketing and public relations.

By 1985, she had become senior vice president of Sebastiani's Hospitality
Department and was charged with managing the company's real estate
holdings. Her husband, Richard Cuneo, who had been an integral part
of Sebastiani winery since 1974, became Chairman of the Board in 2001.

MANGIAMO The Sebastiani Family Cookbook

Bottom: These silver letter openers were one of the first promotional items created by Samuele Sebastiani in the 1930s. Engraved with "Samuele Sebastiani, Fine Wines, Sonoma, CA," these were given to special and potential winery clients in order to emphasize Sebastiani's dedication to quality products.

Right: Branded glasses developed by Samuele Sebastiani, 1937.

In an era when so many wineries are merging with large conglomerates, Sebastiani Vineyards & Winery is proud to have remained family-owned and operated for over 100 years. As Mary Ann puts it, "We are returning to our roots and Samuele's goal to make the finest wines Sonoma has to offer. We are honoring our family's heritage by carrying on the legacy which has been entrusted to us by continuing to set the quality standard for Sonoma winemaking. This winery is like a sibling to us…it's a part of us."

Marc Cuneo, 2005.

IN 2000, A FOURTH GENERATION MEMBER OF THE SEBASTIANI FAMILY—MARY ANN AND RICHARD'S SON, MARC CUNEO— JOINED THE WINERY. Marc is an integral part of the marketing and winemaking teams. He is an ardent outdoorsman who participates in triathalons and tends to his own 20-acre vineyard in Carneros. He received a Bachelor's degree in business from the University of the Pacific in Stockton, California and studied winemaking and viticulture at UC Davis. After working on the bottling line and in the tasting room at Sebastiani, as well as a sales representative for Southern Wines & Spirits, he joined the family business full time as a crush enologist for the 2000 vintage. Now as Vice President of Vineyard Operations and Grower Relations, Marc manages the family's 700 vineyard acres. He also works closely with Sebastiani's contract growers to ensure the quality of the grapes sourced from outside of the estate.

Many of the improvements in wine quality can be traced to changes in the vineyards. Crop loads are smaller and the leaf canopies are better managed to allow for increased sun exposure and riper fruit. Marc states, "We are replanting vineyards and experimenting with rootstock and grape clones. At the winery, wine is made in small lots, with extended extraction time for the reds and a richer regiment of barrel fermentation for the whites." With Sebastiani's new direction and focus, Marc believes that the winery team's passion and culture of continuous innovation make it seem like he's working for a new company, not a 100-year-old family business. "We have dramatically improved the quality of our wines without abandoning value.

Fourth and fifth generation Cuneo and Sebastiani Family members, November 2002.

We over-deliver quality for price by implementing our declassification system. Our winemaker and his team review each wine before bottling. If the wine is not equal to or better in quality than the previous vintage, it is declassified to the tier below or sold off on the bulk market. Due to our declassification system, you could very well be drinking a $17 Cabernet that is made up of $75 wine! Our commitment to excellence results in an elevation of quality throughout the brand. The fact that we can provide a superior-quality bottle of wine at a price reasonable enough for daily enjoyment is what I feel would most please our forefathers. Sebastiani currently produces super-premium wines from Sonoma County, and we truly believe these wines showcase the best Sonoma has to offer. I think if my great-grandfather and my grandfather were alive today, they would be very proud of what Sebastiani Winery has become."

HORS D'OEUVRES

Bagna Cauda, page 31

This dish pairs well with a Sebastiani Chardonnay.

ANCHOVY PUFFS

I package (3 ounces) cream cheese
½ cup butter, softened
I cup flour
I tube (2 ounces) anchovy paste

Mix cheese, butter, and flour well together until it forms a smooth dough. Roll very thin on floured board and cut into 2-inch rounds with a biscuit cutter or a glass. Place about ¼ teaspoon of anchovy paste in center of each round and press together with fingers to form a turnover. Bake in 350 degree oven until slightly brown, about 10 minutes.

ANTIPASTO

6 small artichokes, trimmed and cut in half
I small bunch carrots
I celery heart, cut up small
½ pound string beans, cut up small
I quart white vinegar
I quart water
½ pound peas, fresh or frozen
I small cauliflower, broken in small pieces
I pound small white onions
6 small sweet pickles, drained
I small jar green olives, drained
I small can tomato juice
I cup olive oil
I small can button mushrooms, drained
½ pound small wax peppers
I large can chunk tuna, packed in olive oil
Salt, pepper to taste

Boil artichokes, carrots, celery, and beans for 10 minutes in vinegar and water. Add peas, cauliflower, onions, pickles, and olives and boil for 15 minutes longer. Drain when cooked. Boil tomato juice, oil, and mushrooms. Add drained ingredients to this and let come to a good rolling boil. Salt and pepper to taste. Put into jars along with 1 wax pepper and a piece of tuna. Seal tightly.

ARTICHOKE FRITTATA

Oil from artichoke hearts
3 bunches green onions, chopped
1 clove garlic, chopped
8 eggs
10 soda crackers, crumbled
½ bunch parsley, chopped
1 pound very sharp cheddar cheese, grated
Dash Tabasco sauce
Dash Worcestershire sauce
3 jars (6 ounces each) marinated artichoke hearts, chopped
Salt, pepper to taste

Put oil from artichoke hearts in pan. Fry onions and garlic until limp. Beat eggs in bowl; add cracker crumbs, and beat again. Add parsley, cheese, Tabasco, Worcestershire, and artichokes, beating well after each addition. Season with salt and pepper to taste. When well-blended, put in an oiled 8 x 12 pan and bake at 325 degrees for 35 minutes until firm. Let cool. Cut into strips and wrap each strip separately in plastic wrap and freeze. When ready to serve, thaw and cut into 1 inch squares. Can also be served hot, if you like.

BABY PUFFS

1 cup water
½ cup butter
½ teaspoon salt
1 cup flour
4 eggs

Put water into top of double boiler and boil at medium heat. Add butter and salt; boil until all butter is melted. Put flour in water all at once and reduce heat to low. Stir until mixture leaves sides of pan and coats spoon. Remove from heat and let cool 5 minutes. Break 1 egg at a time into cooled mixture, beating well after each addition until dough gets shiny. Place dough by level teaspoonfuls onto greased cookie sheets. Bake at 400 degrees for 10 minutes, then reduce heat to 350 degrees and let cook for 20 minutes. Turn oven off, let puffs stand in oven with door open for 15 minutes. (This dries the shells out.) Makes about 60 shells which can be filled with your favorite spread or dip.

This recipe for Baby Puffs can also be used for making cream puff shells with the following variations.
1. Place dough on cookie sheet by tablespoonfuls
2. Bake at 450 degrees for 20 minutes. Reduce heat to 350 and bake for 20 minutes.
3. Turn oven off, let shells stand in oven with door open for 15 minutes. Makes 12 shells.
4. See Crab Filling for Baby Buffs below.

CRAB FILLING FOR BABY PUFFS

1 cup fresh crab meat or 1 large can crabmeat, finely chopped
¼ cup chopped parsley
½ cup finely chopped tender celery
1 tablespoon white vinegar
2 tablespoons mayonnaise
½ teaspoon Beau Monde seasoning
White pepper to taste

Mix all ingredients together and stuff into Baby Puffs Shells above.

BAGNA CAUDA

4 celery stalks, cut into strips
2 carrots, cut into strips
1 green bell pepper, cut into strips
¼ pound fresh mushrooms, cut into quarters if large
Italian bread sticks
1 cup heavy cream
4 tablespoons butter
1 can (2 ounces) anchovy filets, drained and finely chopped
1 clove garlic, pressed

Clean and soak celery, carrots, and bell pepper about an hour in cold water to crisp them. Arrange vegetables on platter along with mushrooms and bread sticks. In a heavy saucepan, bring the cream to a boil, stir frequently until thick, and set aside. In a flameproof casserole dish, melt butter over low heat, but do not brown. Add anchovies, garlic, and reserved cream. Do not boil. Serve at once with platter of vegetables and bread sticks.

STUFFED BELGIAN ENDIVE (LETTUCE)

For an interesting variation, cooked artichoke leaves may be used instead of Belgium Endive.

1 cup cooked shrimp or crab
¼ cup mayonnaise
¼ teaspoon dry mustard
1 teaspoon white vinegar
Salt, white pepper, Beau Monde seasoning to taste
Dash of cayenne pepper
1 head Belgian Endive

Combine shrimp or crab with mayonnaise, mustard, and vinegar and season to taste with salt, white pepper, and Beau Monde seasoning, adding a dash of cayenne pepper at the end. Place one teaspoon of this mixture at base of each endive leaf. Arrange on a platter and serve.

BLEU CHEESE BALLS

1 ½ pounds bleu cheese
1 package (8 ounces) cream cheese
1 cube soft butter
1 small onion, finely chopped
1 clove garlic, minced
Cayenne pepper to taste
4 tablespoons Sebastiani Chardonnay or other dry, white wine
½ cup chopped walnuts

Let cheeses and butter warm to room temperature, then beat together until light and well-blended. Add onion, garlic, cayenne pepper, and wine. Chill until manageable to roll into balls. After forming balls, roll them in nuts until well-covered. Serve on a tray with your favorite crackers.

SPARKLING WINE BLEU CHEESE SPREAD

½ pound bleu cheese
½ pound butter
Cayenne pepper to taste
½ cup sparkling wine
¼ cup brandy

Blend cheese, butter, and cayenne into a smooth paste. Moisten with sparkling wine and brandy and serve with crackers or any fresh bread.

CANTALOUPE CUBES

8 slices prosciutto
1 medium cantaloupe

Cut prosciutto into 1 inch strips. Cut cantaloupe into cubes. Wrap strips of prosciutto around each cantaloupe cube and secure with toothpick. Serve chilled.

For another variation, use smoked salmon strips and wrap around cubes of honeydew melon. When melons are out of season, use cubes of avocado or papaya and top with a sprinkling of black pepper.

Cantaloupe Cubes, opposite page

CLAM DIP

2 cans minced clams
½ cup clam juice
4 jars Borden's very sharp cheddar cheese
¾ bunch green onions, chopped
1 small clove garlic, chopped
6 shakes paprika
1 tablespoon Worcestershire sauce
6 shakes Tabasco sauce
5 tablespoons chopped parsley

Blend all ingredients together and bake in uncovered casserole for 20 minutes at 350 degrees. Reduce heat to 200 degrees and let bake for 45 minutes. Serve in chafing dish. Toasted bread, crackers, or Melba toast are excellent with this dip.

MINCED CLAM CANAPÉS

Makes about 3 dozen

About 36 bread rounds, 1¾ inch in diameter
1 package (8 ounces) cream cheese
1 tablespoon Worcestershire sauce
2 to 3 dashes cayenne pepper
¼ teaspoon salt
2 teaspoons grated onion
1 can minced clams, drained
Grated Parmesan cheese
Paprika

Toast bread rounds on one side. Cream cheese with Worcestershire, cayenne pepper, salt, onion, and clams. Heap mixture by teaspoons on untoasted side of bread rounds. Sprinkle over top with cheese and paprika. Place under broiler half way down in oven so that they will cook and brown slowly. Broil until lightly brown, about 5 minutes and serve hot.

CRAB OR SHRIMP DIP

3 packages (8 ounces each) cream cheese
3 large cans king crab or shrimp
Dash garlic salt
½ cup mayonnaise
2 teaspoons prepared mustard
1 teaspoon dry mustard
1 tablespoon lemon juice
¼ cup Sebastiani Chardonnay or other dry, white wine
2 teaspoons powdered sugar
1 teaspoon onion juice
Dash of salt
2 dashes cayenne pepper

Melt cream cheese in top of double boiler. Add remaining ingredients and mix well. May be served hot or cold. Also freezes well.

HOT CRAB CHEESE SPREAD

1 package (8 ounces) cream cheese
1 tablespoon light cream
2 tablespoons Worcestershire sauce
1 teaspoon lemon juice
Dash of cayenne pepper
1 can (7 ½ ounces) crabmeat
2 tablespoons chopped green onion
Slivered almonds, toasted

Combine cheese, cream, Worcestershire, lemon juice, and cayenne. Drain crab and wash thoroughly with cold running water. Drain again. Add crab and onion to cheese mixture. Turn mixture into a buttered shallow baking pan and sprinkle with almonds. Bake at 350 degrees for 15 minutes. (Can be frozen if you wish.)

CRABMEAT CANAPÉS

We recommend Sebastiani
Chardonnay with this hors d'oeuvre.

3 tablespoons butter
3 tablespoons flour
½ cup cream
½ cup chicken stock
¼ cup Sebastiani Chardonnay or other dry, white wine
2 tablespoons minced parsley
1 teaspoon minced onion
1 cup crabmeat, fresh or canned
60 rounds (1 ½ inch) white bread
Grated Parmesan cheese
Paprika
Salt, garlic salt, pepper to taste

Melt butter and stir in flour. Add cream and chicken stock. Cook, stirring constantly, until thick. Remove from heat and add wine, parsley, onion, crab, and seasonings to taste. Chill thoroughly. Toast rounds of bread on cookie sheet (only on one side). Spread untoasted side with crab mixture. Sprinkle with cheese and paprika. Broil until browned. Serve at once.

STUFFED EGGS

6 hard-cooked eggs
4 tablespoons soft butter
3 tablespoons mayonnaise
2 teaspoons minced onion
1 teaspoon prepared mustard
½ teaspoon white vinegar
1 teaspoon garlic salt
Dash of cayenne pepper
Mayonnaise
Parsley sprigs

Halve eggs, remove yolks, and mash yolks with fork, reserving egg whites for stuffing. Mix them with butter, mayonnaise, onion, mustard, vinegar, and seasonings. Fill reserved egg whites, garnish with a dab of mayonnaise and tiny sprig of parsley on top of each egg half.

EGGS STUFFED WITH CHICKEN

6 hard-cooked eggs
¼ cup cooked, finely chopped chicken
3 teaspoons mayonnaise
2 teaspoons white vinegar
½ teaspoon prepared mustard
Dash of cayenne pepper
Parsley
Paprika
Salt, garlic salt to taste

Halve whole eggs, remove yolks, and mash yolks with chicken, reserving egg whites for stuffing. Add mayonnaise, vinegar, mustard, cayenne pepper, salt, and garlic salt, adding more mayonnaise if necessary to attain creamy texture. Fill reserved egg whites with chicken mixture and garnish each with a dot of mayonnaise and a sprinkling each of parsley and paprika.

STUFFED FRENCH ROLLS

1 pound salami, ground or finely chopped
2 jars creamy sharp cheddar spread
¼ to ½ cup Sebastiani Zinfandel or other dry, red wine
6 to 8 sour French rolls

Mix salami, cheese spread, and wine together in a bowl. With a knife, remove centers from French rolls and stuff with salami mixture. Chill overnight and slice before serving.

BROILED STUFFED MUSHROOMS

1 pound mushrooms
2 or 3 green onions, finely chopped
3 tablespoons butter
¼ cup bread crumbs
¼ cup chopped parsley
¼ teaspoon oregano
¼ teaspoon salt
Few grains cayenne pepper
3 tablespoons grated Parmesan cheese
2 teaspoons Sebastiani Chardonnay or other dry, white wine
Butter or oil for brushing
Paprika

Wash mushrooms and drain well. Remove stems and chop finely. Sauté mushrooms and onions in butter. Add remaining ingredients and heat until warm. Brush mushroom caps lightly with butter or oil. Press stuffing into caps, sprinkle with paprika, and heat under broiler until mushrooms are tender, about 5 minutes.

ROSA ANGELINA'S HOT MEXICAN CHEESE DIP

2 pounds Kraft Velveeta cheese
1 can cheddar cheese soup
1 can (10 ounces) chilies and tomatoes, chopped
1 teaspoon garlic salt
1 teaspoon onion salt
1 teaspoon Salsa Jalapena*

Cut Velveeta into cubes and melt in top of double boiler. Add soup and tomatoes and blend. Add garlic salt, onion salt, and Salsa Jalapena, stirring well. Use tortilla triangles to dip.

* Salsa Jalapena, a commercially-prepared sauce, is very hot, so use your own judgment as to quantity.

LIVER PÂTÉ

This pâté is the perfect companion to a glass of Sebastiani Eye of the Swan.

1 pound chicken livers
1 bay leaf
3 stalks celery, sliced
1 cube soft butter
3 ounces Brandy
1 tablespoon dry mustard
Salt, onion salt, pepper to taste

Boil livers in salted water with bay leaf and celery. Drain livers well and chop, and cream with butter, brandy, and mustard. Add seasonings to taste. Spread on crackers for an exccllent hors d' oeuvre.

MEAT BALLS

Serves 6–8

Try a Sebastiani Barbera with this appetizer.

¾ pound ground beef
¼ pound ground pork
¼ cup bread crumbs, soft
1 egg
2 tablespoons grated onion
1 teaspoon lemon juice
½ teaspoon salt
½ teaspoon pepper
½ teaspoon Accent seasoning
Oil
½ cup plain applesauce
½ cup water
½ cup ketchup

Mix beef, pork, bread crumbs, egg, onion, lemon juice, and seasonings together in a bowl. Form meatball mixture into ½ inch balls. Brown meat balls in a little oil; add applesauce, water, and ketchup. Pour into greased baking dish and bake 30 minutes at 350 degrees. Place into chafing dish to keep warm while serving.

OLIVE-CHEESE BALLS

Serve with Sebastiani Symphony.

1 cup grated sharp cheddar cheese
2 tablespoons butter
½ cup flour
Dash of cayenne pepper
1 clove garlic, pressed (optional)
25 medium black or green olives, pitted and drained
Salt, pepper to taste

Cream cheese and butter together. Add flour, cayenne pepper, garlic, and salt and pepper to taste. Wrap a teaspoonful of this mixture around each olive making a ball. Bake for 15 minutes at 400 degrees. Serve the olive-cheese balls with cocktail picks.

PROSCIUTTO AND BREAD STICKS

Prosciutto, very thinly sliced
Bread sticks, 4 inches long

Cut prosciutto into 1 to 1 ½ inch strips and wrap around individual bread sticks and serve.

SHRIMP MOUSSE

This is an excellent hors d'oeuvre to serve before any type of meal as a cracker spread. It may also be used as a salad.

1 envelope unflavored gelatin
¼ cup cold water
¾ cup Sebastiani Chardonnay or other dry, white wine
1 can (7 ounces) shrimp
1 tablespoon chopped onion
1 teaspoon lemon juice
½ teaspoon dry mustard
Salt, white pepper to taste
Dash of cayenne pepper
1 cup mayonnaise
Several lettuce leaves
Few sprigs parsley (optional)
Lemon peel (optional)

Soften gelatin in water. Heat wine and stir in gelatin until dissolved. Set aside and cool thoroughly. Put shrimp, onion, lemon juice, mustard, and seasonings in blender; add mayonnaise and blend until smooth. Stir in cooled wine mixture and pour into mold. Chill until firm. Unmold on cold platter garnished with lettuce. Decorate with parsley and lemon peel if desired.

Shrimp Soup, page 48

SOUPS

soup tips

1. Homemade soups seem to have gone out of style because so many people will not take time to do the job. But they really aren't that complicated or time-consuming.

2. I like to serve a soup course instead of a salad occasionally for luncheons or dinners.

3. A thick soup like minestrone, can be served as a main course for lunch.

4. Soup can be made one day and served the next. It is always tasty when re-heated.

5 Many times I make large quantities of soup which I freeze in quart jars or milk cartons. This saves a great amount of work and provides quick, easy meals.

6. To easily remove fat from soups, place serveral ice cubes in a cloth, tie ends together, and skim surface of soup.

7. Always heat soup plates or cups and serve hot.

BEEF-PEARL BARLEY SOUP

When fresh vegetables are in season, add 6 string beans, chopped and ½ cup peas. Carrots can be added to the soup, also, but my husband always said they made the soup too sweet. This soup will taste better heated over the next day, and it can also be frozen as this recipe makes a large quantity.

1 chuck roast (2 pounds; or 3 beef shanks)
1 gallon boiling water
1 can whole packed tomatoes or 3 fresh peeled tomatoes, chopped
½ cup pearl barley
2 to 3 teaspoons salt
1 teaspoon garlic salt
½ teaspoon pepper
1 small red chili pepper (optional)
2 cloves garlic, finely chopped (optional)
2 zucchini, unpeeled and chopped
1 teaspoon chopped basil
3 tablespoons chopped parsley
½ cup Sebastiani Chardonnay or other dry, white wine
Grated Parmesan cheese

Trim all fat from meat and put into boiling water. Add tomatoes and barley. If using fresh tomatoes, add ½ teaspoon sugar. Add remaining ingredients and simmer at least 2 ½ hours. Taste soup when it has cooked 1 ½ hours—you may want to add more salt. When meat is tender, remove from pot and slice into strips. Serve as an accompaniment to soup with ketchup and mustard. Sprinkle cheese over soup before serving.

BUTTER BALL SOUP

Serves 4–6

1 ½ loaves stale white bread, sliced
1 cube soft butter
3 eggs
Salt, white pepper to taste
4 to 6 cups chicken broth
2 teaspoons chopped parsley
½ cup uncooked rice (optional)

Remove crusts from bread slices and crumble insides between hands. Add butter, eggs, salt, and white pepper. Mix well and knead until mixture can be formed into small balls. Form balls ¾ inch in diameter and drop into boiling chicken broth. Sprinkle with parsley and add rice, if desired. Cook until rice is tender and serve.

CHICKEN SOUP

Makes about 1 ½ quarts

1 boiling chicken
3 quarts boiling water
2 celery stalks
1 onion, whole
1 clove garlic
2 sprigs parsley
2 to 3 coils capellini or pastina
Grated Parmesan cheese
Salt, white pepper to taste

Place chicken into deep kettle of boiling water along with celery, onion, garlic, parsley, salt, and white pepper. Skim surface occasionally to remove grease while cooking over medium low heat for 2 to 2 ½ hours. Remove chicken and cut into pieces. Strain broth and add capellini. Cook 5 to 10 minutes longer and sprinkle with cheese before serving.

This recipe yields quite a large amount of butter ball mixture. Use as much as you desire, then chill or freeze the rest for use on another day.

A tradition in our family is to serve this when someone isn't feeling well as it is very easily digested. Be sure to use only very fine capellini or pastina for this recipe and, if desired, a few egg yolks may also be dropped into the chicken broth.

Serve with a Sebastiani Chardonnay.

MANGIAMO The Sebastiani Family Cookbook

CHICKEN FEET SOUP

10 chicken feet
6 chicken wings
2 quarts water
2 teaspoons salt
2 stalks celery
1 onion
1 clove garlic
¼ to ½ cup pastina (fine paste), cooked according to directions on package
Salt, pepper to taste

Scald chicken feet in salted boiling water, then remove skins and nails. Return to 2 quarts fresh boiling water and add wings, vegetables, and garlic. Let boil an additional 1 to 2 hours. Then strain and season to taste with salt and pepper. Serve soup with a fine pastina and place chicken parts onto a separate platter to serve.

If available, chicken necks may also be added to the soup. Add to boiling water along with chicken wings and vegetables.

CLAM CHOWDER

1 onion, sliced or chopped
2 tablespoons butter
3 to 4 slices bacon, cut into pieces
Salt to taste
⅛ teaspoon pepper
4 cups diced potatoes
1 quart minced clams, reserve liquid
4 cups milk

Sauté onion with butter and bacon. Add salt and pepper. Add cubed potatoes, reserved clam liquid, and water enough to cover. Cook until nearly tender. Add milk and boil; when potatoes are cooked, add clams and cook only 3 minutes longer.

If you prefer tomato clam chowder, substitute tomato sauce for the milk called for in the recipe.

CRAB OR SHRIMP SOUP

Serves 4

3 tablespoons butter
3 tablespoons flour
3 cups milk
¼ teaspoon garlic salt
½ teaspoon salt
¼ teaspoon white pepper
8–10 ounces shrimp or crab (more if you like)
1 teaspoon chopped parsley

In top of double boiler, melt butter and add flour. Add milk gradually and cook until thick. Add garlic salt, salt, and white pepper. Cover and keep on low heat. Just before serving, add shellfish and parsley.

EGG SOUP

4 eggs
2 tablespoons fine semolina
3 scant tablespoons Parmesan cheese, grated
1 cup cold chicken broth
2 ½ quarts rich chicken broth
Salt, pepper to taste

Beat eggs, semolina, and Parmesan well in a bowl. Slowly blend in cold chicken broth, beating continuously with a whisk until smooth and without lumps. Bring rich chicken broth to a boil and pour egg mixture all at once into the boiling broth. Reduce heat to a simmer and stir vigorously for 3 to 4 minutes until slightly flaky. Season with salt and pepper.

Enjoy with a bottle of Sebastiani Pinot Noir.

FARINATA

Serves 4

This is a truly different and delicious soup.

3 ½ cups chicken broth
1 clove garlic, pressed
2 teaspoons chopped parsley
2 tablespoons polenta
4 leaves escarole, cut into 1 inch strips (romaine lettuce or kale may be used instead)

Bring broth to boil. Add garlic, parsley, and polenta. Let simmer, covered, for 40 minutes. Add lettuce and cook 10 minutes longer (if kale is used, cook an additional 10 minutes).

MEATBALL SOUP

Makes 3 quarts

Meatballs:
½ pound ground beef
¼ cup uncooked oatmeal
½ small onion, finely chopped
1 clove garlic, pressed
2 tablespoons grated Parmesan cheese
1 teaspoon chopped parsley
¼ teaspoon garlic salt
½ teaspoon salt
⅛ teaspoon pepper
2 tablespoons tomato sauce
1 ½ teaspoons Sebastiani Cabernet Sauvignon or Zinfandel or other
    dry, red wine
1 egg, beaten

Broth:
2 quarts boiling water
2 teaspoons salt
1 teaspoon garlic salt
2 stalks tender celery, finely chopped

Recipe continued on following page

2 teaspoons chopped parsley

1 small onion, chopped

1 teaspoon chopped basil (optional)

2 celery leaves, chopped (optional)

4 tablespoons tomato sauce

½ cup uncooked rice

Grated Parmesan cheese

Combine all meatball ingredients together and mix well. Form into small balls. In a large pot of boiling water, add seasonings, all vegetables, and tomato sauce. Then add meatballs. Let simmer 45 minutes. Add rice and let simmer another 20 minutes. Sprinkle with cheese before serving.

QUICK MINESTRONE

Serves 6

1 can (11 ounces) red kidney beans

1 teaspoon salt

½ teaspoon garlic salt

1 clove garlic, pressed

¼ teaspoon pepper

1 tablespoon oil

¼ cup chopped parsley

1 small zucchini, unpeeled and cut into small cubes

2 stalks celery, chopped

1 small carrot, diced

2 green onions, chopped

4 to 5 leaves Swiss chard, chopped

3 tablespoons butter

1 can (8 ounces) tomato sauce or 1 can solid packed tomatoes, mashed

2 ½ cups water

½ cup Sebastiani Chardonnay or other dry, white wine

¼ cup uncooked elbow macaroni (optional)

Grated Parmesan cheese

Place undrained beans in a large kettle or saucepan; mash about ⅔ of the beans and leave the rest whole. Add salt, garlic salt, garlic, pepper, oil, and parsley,

Recipe continued on following page

Minestrone is an old recipe that used to take about half a day to prepare, starting with dry, red beans. This is a modern version using canned kidney beans, and it is equally as good as the old. I usually serve it with garlic bread and a salad and this makes a very nourishing meal. If available, several leaves of fresh basil, chopped finely, will give added flavor. Sometimes, I also add ½ cup grated or cubed potatoes. The longer the minestrone is cooked, the better the flavor.

Minestrone pairs well with a glass of Sebastiani Barbera.

Quick Minestrone, opposite page

stirring well. Then add all the vegetables, butter, tomato sauce, and water. Simmer 1 hour or more and then add wine. (If desired, macaroni may be added at this point.) Simmer 10 to 15 minutes longer. Sprinkle with cheese before serving. If soup seems too thick, add more water and salt to taste.

OYSTER SOUP

Serves 4

2 tablespoons butter
1 cup finely chopped celery
2 tablespoons flour
1 pint milk
1 pint stewing oysters
2 teaspoons chopped parsley
4 teaspoons Sebastiani Chardonnay or other dry, white wine
Salt, paprika to taste

Simmer butter and celery in top of double boiler until tender. Blend in flour. Add milk and seasoning, stirring well. Clean oysters and chop finely. When ready to serve soup, add oysters, parsley, and wine to taste. Heat thoroughly, but do not overcook. Keep covered when not stirring.

RAVIOLI OR TORTELLINI IN BROTH

4 cups canned chicken broth
24 ravioli or tortellini
2 teaspoons chopped parsley
Grated Parmesan cheese

Bring chicken broth to boil and add ravioli or tortellini. Cook until tender, about 15 minutes. Sprinkle with parsley and grated cheese before serving.

This soup makes a fine first course for dinner. It's soup and pasta all in one!

RICE-MILK SOUP

Serves 4

4 cups milk
½ cup uncooked rice
1 teaspoon salt

In top of a double boiler, bring milk to just under boiling. Add rice and salt and stir frequently. Cook, covered, 30 minutes, and stir occasionally until rice is tender.

SPLIT PEA SOUP

Serves 6

Serve with a Sebastiani Eye of the Swan.

1 ½ cups split peas
Ham bone
½ onion, finely chopped
1 cup finely chopped celery
6 cups boiling water
1 clove garlic, chopped
Dash of cayenne
2 tablespoons butter
2 tablespoons flour
Paprika
Salt to taste

Add peas, ham bone, onion, and celery to boiling water. Then add garlic and cayenne. Simmer, covered, for 2 hours. Put the soup through a sieve. Chill and remove grease. Melt butter and stir in flour until well-blended. Add a little of the soup mixture slowly. Cook and stir until it boils then add to the rest of the soup. Season soup with salt and paprika.

Pasta con Pesto, page 60

PASTA & RICE

pasta & rice tips

1. When boiling pasta, add one teaspoon of salt for every four cups of water, the pasta will not stick together.

2. A tablespoon of vinegar added to homemade noodles will keep them from being tough.

3. A few drops of lemon juice added to rice while it is boiling will keep the grains separated and make the rice whiter.

BAKED LASAGNA

Serves 8

1 package (12 ounces) lasagna noodles
1 pound ricotta cheese (optional)
½ pound mozzarella cheese, sliced thinly
½ pound Swiss cheese, grated
Spaghetti Sauce (see recipe on page 72)
Grated Parmesan cheese
Salt, pepper to taste

Cook lasagna noodles in boiling, salted water, adding a few drops of olive oil to the water. Cook as directed on package and drain immediately. Immerse noodles in cold water. In a greased, shallow casserole dish, arrange a layer of lasagna. Spread a layer of ricotta over this, then a layer of spaghetti sauce, then a layer of mozzarella, topping all with a sprinkling of Swiss cheese. Repeat layers in this order until all ingredients are used, ending with a layer of sauce and a sprinkling of grated Parmesan. Bake at 350 degrees for 50 minutes. Remove from oven and let stand about 15 minutes so that it will be easy to cut.

I have made ricotta cheese optional in this recipe as I have found that the lasagna is good even without it.

We recommend serving a bottle of Sebastiani Zinfandel.

CANELLONI

Serves 8

1 package (8 ounces) canelloni
Spaghetti Sauce (see recipe on page 72)

Meat Filling:
1 medium onion, chopped
4 tablespoons olive oil
1 ½ pounds ground beef
2 tablespoons chopped parsley
2 eggs, slightly beaten
¼ pound mozzarella cheese, diced
¼ pound Swiss cheese, grated
1 cup bread crumbs
⅔ cup milk
Salt, pepper to taste

Place up to 8 canelloni in 6 quarts boiling water. Cook for 5 minutes only. Remove carefully with strainer spoon. Run cold water over shells until cool enough to handle. Make meat filling by first sautéing onion in oil. Add ground meat and season while meat cooks. When well-browned remove from heat and let cool. Mix in parsley, eggs, cheeses, bread crumbs, and milk. Fill canelloni, using a butter knife; then refrigerate until ready to use. When ready to bake, cover bottom of a baking dish with spaghetti sauce. Lay canelloni in side by side and cover with sauce. Cover dish with aluminum foil, crimping edges to seal. Bake in 400 degree oven for 40 minutes. Remove foil and bake another 10 minutes.

When I have a small fresh Italian sausage on hand, I break it into very small pieces and mix it with the beef prior to browning. It adds considerably to the flavor of the filling.

Try some Sebastiani Barbera with this pasta.

CLAMS WITH PASTA

Serves 4

½ cup butter
2 cloves garlic, chopped
½ cup Sebastiani Chardonnay or other dry, white wine
1 can (7 ½ ounces) minced clams, drain and reserve liquid
1 package (12 ounces) large pasta shells
2 tablespoons chopped parsley
Salt, pepper to taste

Melt butter in heavy skillet, stir in garlic, and cook over medium heat for a few minutes. Do not let garlic brown. Add wine and reserved clam liquid and simmer 5 to 6 minutes. Remove from heat and set aside. Boil pasta shells as indicated on package and drain well. Transfer to a heated serving dish. Return sauce to heat and bring to a boil over high heat. Add the clams and cook until the clams are thoroughly heated. Pour over shells, sprinkle top with parsley, and toss together until all ingredients are well-mixed. Season to taste with salt and pepper.

DOUGH FOR EGG PASTA

4 cups flour
3 eggs, slightly beaten
2 teaspoons salt
2 tablespoons olive oil
¼ to ½ cup lukewarm water

Sift flour onto a large pastry board. Make a well in the center and put in slightly-beaten eggs. Add salt and oil and mix flour into eggs, a little at a time. Add water a few drops at a time just enough to make the dough soft enough to knead. Knead dough on floured board with the heel of the hand for 10 to 12 minutes until it is smooth and elastic. Roll out and cut into desired shapes and sizes for use in recipe of your choice, flour gently, and let dry for at least 1 hour before cooking. May be used for any dish calling for pasta, (e.g., spaghetti, lasagna, fettucine).

PASTA CON PESTO

Serves 4

Pesto:

2 cups coarsely chopped fresh basil leaves
1 to 2 sprigs parsley
1 teaspoon salt
½ teaspoon pepper
2 cloves garlic
1 cup olive oil
½ cup grated Parmesan cheese

Pasta:

6 ounces spaghetti rings (or your favorite pasta)
1 medium potato, peeled and cut (or small new potatoes, if available)
1 small zucchini, cut into ½ inch rounds (or a few cut-up Italian beans, when in season)
2 tablespoons olive oil

Combine basil, parsley, salt, pepper, garlic, and oil in blender. Blend just a few seconds. Stop blender and push herbs down with a rubber spatula. Blend a few seconds, then stop again to push herbs down. Repeat this procedure until sauce is fairly thin, but not liquefied. Transfer sauce to a bowl and add cheese and reserve. Cook pasta, potatoes, and zucchini in salted, boiling water, but not too vigorously. Add olive oil, then drain thoroughly, reserving 1 cup of this liquid. Add a little liquid to pesto and pour 4 to 5 tablespoons pesto over pasta and toss until all pasta is well-coated. The remaining pesto may be refrigerated or frozen for future use.

FETTUCINE

Serves about 6

½ cup soft butter
¼ cup heavy cream
½ cup grated Parmesan cheese
6 to 8 quarts water
1 tablespoon salt
1 pound cooked fettucine
Salt, pepper to taste

Cream butter until light and fluffy. Beat in cream a little at a time, then add cheese by the tablespoon, beating well after each addition. Cook fettucine in salted, boiling water as indicated on package. Drain immediately and thoroughly. Transfer at once to a hot serving bowl. Add butter-cheese mixture to fettucine and toss until all fettucine is well-coated. Taste and season with salt and pepper. Serve at once with additional cheese.

POTATO GNOCCHI (LOMBARD-STYLE)

Serves 6–8

6 large potatoes, hot and cooked
4 tablespoons butter
3 eggs, slightly beaten
2 teaspoons baking powder
4 cups flour
¼ cup melted butter
½ cup grated Parmesan cheese
Salt, white pepper to taste

For people who like the flavor of garlic, follow the directions, except mince two cloves of garlic and add to the melted butter, browning lightly. Pour over cooked gnocchi and add cheese. Spaghetti Sauce (recipe on page 72) may also be used as an accompaniment to gnocchi. Simply pour the sauce over the gnocchi in the baking dish and let bake a few minutes. Serve with cheese.

This gnocchi is delicious with a bottle of Sebastiani Barbera.

Mash potatoes. Beat in butter, eggs, and baking powder. Salt and white pepper to taste. Sift in flour, making a stiff dough. Mix and knead until dough is smooth. Shape dough into long rolls about as thick as a finger and cut into 1 inch pieces. Pressing with thumb, roll each gnocchi over the back of a fork. (An easier method is to press each piece with your thumb to make a crescent shape.) Cook gnocchi a few at a time in a large pot of boiling, salted water until they rise to the

Recipe continued on following page

surface about 10 minutes. Remove gently and repeat until all gnocchi are cooked. Arrange in a heated baking dish and sprinkle generously with melted butter and cheese. Set the dish in a 350 degree oven for a few minutes until cheese melts.

PASTA FOR GREEN NOODLES

Serves 8–10

½ pound spinach
4 cups flour
2 teaspoons salt
2 tablespoons olive oil
2 eggs, well-beaten
Spaghetti Sauce (see recipe on page 72)

Cook spinach, drain well, and put through a fine-meshed sieve. Sift flour and salt onto a large pastry board. Make a well in the center and put in oil, eggs, and spinach. Using the fingers, mix well until all ingredients are blended. If necessary, add a few drops of water so that all flour is mixed in. If pasta becomes too soft, add more flour. Knead thoroughly for at least 12 minutes until pasta is smooth and elastic. Divide dough into fourths and roll out each fourth about ¹⁄₁₆ inch thick. Roll up each sheet, cut cross-wise into strips of desired width. Let dry for 30 minutes. Use with spaghetti sauce.

PIZZA BREAD DOUGH

1 package fresh yeast
2 tablespoons lukewarm water
1 cup boiling water
1 ½ teaspoons salt
2 tablespoons butter
3 cups sifted flour

Crumble yeast in water for 5 minutes. Pour boiling water over salt and butter, let cool to lukewarm, then add yeast. Add half of flour and beat smooth. Then add remaining flour and beat smooth again. Divide dough in half for this pizza. Use all of dough for thicker pizza. Place dough on floured board and pat gently

Recipe continued on following page

into 1 (14 inch) round or 2 (11 inch) rounds, with edges slightly thicker. Place on greased cookie sheet. Let rise in warm place (85 degrees) until dough doubles in height. Arrange filling on top and bake as directed in Pizza Filling recipe below.

PIZZA FILLING

3 tablespoons olive oil
½ cup grated Parmesan cheese
¾ pound mozzarella cheese, sliced
2 cups canned tomatoes, diced, peeled and drained
1 clove garlic, minced
½ teaspoon salt
⅛ teaspoon pepper
½ teaspoon dried oregano or thyme

Prepare Pizza Bread Dough on previous page. After dough rises, brush with 1 tablespoon oil. Sprinkle with Parmesan; arrange ¹/₃ mozzarella on top. Sprinkle with tomatoes mixed with garlic, salt, and pepper. Arrange remaining mozzarella on top. Sprinkle with oregano, then sprinkle on 2 tablespoons oil. Bake in 450 degree oven 25 to 30 minutes until crust is golden brown.

There are many variations for pizza. Here are just a few:

Anchovy Pizza: Make pizza as above and dot anchovies from a 2 ounce can of anchovy filets, finely minced. Drizzle on oil from anchovies and garnish with a few slices of green pepper. Bake as directed.

Mushroom Pizza: Make basic pizza. Sprinkle on top 1/4 pound chopped mushrooms, sautéed in 2 tablespoons olive oil with 1/4 teaspoon salt for 5 minutes. Bake as directed.

Sausage Pizza: Make basic pizza. Dot surface with thin slices of one Italian sausage from which the skin has been removed. Bake as directed. To prevent tearing pizza, cut with kitchen shears.

Pizza pairs perfectly with a Sebastiani Zinfandel.

MALFATTI

Serves 12

Malfattis are for the adventurous cook since they are a bit tricky. If desired, malfatti can be prepared the day before and arranged in a baking dish with spaghetti sauce poured over all. Simply refrigerate overnight and heat before serving in a slow oven until heated thoroughly.

2 packages frozen spinach
½ loaf dry French bread
1 medium onion, finely chopped
1 clove garlic, finely chopped
1 teaspoon salt
¼ teaspoon pepper
1 to 2 cups dry bread crumbs
1 cup grated Parmesan cheese
½ cup parsley, finely chopped
1 teaspoon basil, finely chopped
3 to 4 eggs
Spaghetti Sauce (see recipe on page 72)
Grated Parmesan cheese

Cook frozen spinach in frying pan with a little water. Squeeze dry and chop finely. Soak bread in hot water and squeeze dry. Sauté onion and garlic, adding salt and pepper. Mix together spinach, bread, onion, and garlic. (If possible, use a meat grinder for this process.) Mix in bread crumbs, cheese, parsley, and basil. Break in eggs and mix well. Season to taste. Take small amount of mixture into floured hands and roll into links like pork sausage. Drop into boiling, salted water. When the malfattis float to the surface, they are done. Remove a few at a time gently, let drain, and serve with spaghetti sauce and grated cheese.

MOCK RAVIOLI

Serves 10–12

If desired, half of this may be frozen for another meal. Serve with a Sebastiani Merlot.

1 pound ground round
1 onion, chopped
1 clove garlic
1 tablespoon olive oil
1 small can tomato sauce
1 ½ cups water
1 teaspoon mixed Italian herbs
1 teaspoon fresh thyme
½ cup dry Italian mushrooms
½ pound butterfly macaroni
Salt, pepper to taste

Spinach Mixture:
1 ½ cups frozen spinach, chopped and cooked
½ cup bread crumbs
½ cup chopped parsley
½ cup grated Parmesan cheese
1 clove garlic, chopped
¼ cup olive oil
1 teaspoon salt
1 teaspoon sage
4 eggs, well-beaten

Brown meat, onion, and garlic in oil, adding garlic last. Season with salt and pepper, then add tomato sauce, water, herbs, thyme, and mushrooms. Let simmer 10 minutes. Cook butterfly macaroni in salted, boiling water as indicated on package. Prepare spinach mixture by combining all ingredients together and mixing well, making sure that spinach is drained thoroughly before using. Grease a deep, large (8 x 10) casserole dish. Put a layer of macaroni at bottom of casserole, then spread a layer of spinach mixture over this. Top with a layer of meat mixture. Continue in this manner until dish is full, topping with macaroni and meat sauce. Bake at 350 degrees for 40 minutes.

Serve with a Sebastiani Zinfandel.

NONI PINI'S RAVIOLI

Dough:

4 cups flour
1 egg
2 tablespoons olive oil
2 teaspoons salt
1 cup warm water

Filling:

1 chicken breast
1 ½ pounds ground round or veal
1 set beef brains
3 tablespoons butter
2 cloves garlic, finely chopped
1 ½ bunches spinach
¼ cup chopped parsley
½ cup grated Parmesan cheese
¼ cup grated Swiss cheese
3 eggs, slightly beaten
Salt, pepper to taste

Mix all dough ingredients together and knead for about 20 minutes. Test by pressing finger into dough; when it bounces back, it is ready. Let dough stand about 10 minutes in a covered bowl to rise. Divide dough in half. Roll out one half into a round, letting half of this hang over the edge of the board. Roll out the rest of the dough away from you twice. Stretch dough and then roll it twice side to side, keeping it tight under the pin. Reverse dough and roll the other half in the same manner, flouring lightly as you do. Roll until dough is $1/16$ inch thick. Repeat procedure for other half of dough. Let dry 1 hour or place on cookie sheets and freeze overnight. (This makes the dough easier to work with.)

Dice chicken, ground round, and brains. Melt butter in skillet; add meats, sauté lightly. Then add garlic. Salt and pepper to taste. Sauté until meat is tender, then chop finely. Wash spinach thoroughly and cook for 5 minutes. Drain well and chop finely. Add salt and pepper to taste. Combine chopped meats, spinach, and parsley with cheese and eggs. Makes about 4 cups of filling, enough for 250 small raviolis.

Recipe continued on following page

Preparing Ravioli:
Take one layer of dough and spread half of meat mixture over one half of the dough's surface. Fold other half over and roll with a ravioli rolling pin. Then cut with a ravioli cutter. Repeat process with remaining dough and meat mixture. Boil raviolis in salted, boiling water 10 to 15 minutes until tender when pricked with a fork. Raviolis can be kept frozen up to 4 weeks.

POLENTA CASSEROLE

Serves 6–8

3 quarts water (reduce water, if thicker polenta is desired)
1 ½ tablespoons salt
3 cups polenta
½ cube butter
Spaghetti Sauce (see recipe on page 72)
Grated Parmesan cheese
1 pound Teleme or cheddar cheese, shredded (optional)

Bring water to a boil; add salt. Measure polenta into a bowl and add gradually into water. Stir constantly. Turn heat down and continue stirring frequently for 50 minutes. Butter a shallow casserole dish and spread half the polenta in bottom. Put Spaghetti Sauce and cheese over this, then spread another layer of polenta, again topping with sauce and cheese. Slices of Teleme cheese can be used between the layers, if desired. Bake in 375 degree oven for 30 minutes.

Polenta, a terribly-neglected dish, is very delicious and has many variations. It can be served with Venison Stew, Beef Stew, Pheasant Cacciatore, Chicken Cacciatore, or boiled Italian sausage (see recipes in this book). Simply cook polenta and serve with the various dishes poured over it on individual plates. For those who like cheese, sprinkle with grated parmesan. I have learned to cook polenta in a pressure cooker and it works very well. Using 1 cup less water and only 1 tablespoon salt, cook according to pressure cooker directions for 20 minutes. If any polenta is left over, we put the polenta in a bowl and refrigerate. The next day it can be sliced approximately ½ inch thick and fried in oil and butter mixed with a touch of garlic salt. Cook until crusty and serve. Another way to use leftover polenta is to slice it as above and put slices in a buttered shallow baking dish. Top with thin slices of Monterey cheese and bake in a slow oven until cheese melts. Serve immediately.

RICE CASSEROLE

Serves 4

1 tablespoon chopped onion
1 tablespoon oil
1 tablespoon butter
1 clove garlic, pressed or finely chopped
1 can solid pack tomatoes, mashed
1 cup raw rice
½ cup Sebastiani Chardonnay or other dry, white wine
1 to 2 cups leftover meat, cubed (any kind will do)
Grated Parmesan cheese
Salt, pepper to taste

Brown onion in oil and butter, adding a little salt and pepper. Add garlic and sauté briefly. Then add tomatoes, rice, wine, and meat. Salt and pepper to taste. Cover and bake 40 minutes in 350 degree oven. Sprinkle with cheese just before serving.

RICE TORTE

For a variation, add chopped green peppers instead of the zucchini.

7 eggs, slightly beaten
2 cups cooked rice
2 medium zucchini, shredded
½ cup olive oil
1 cup grated Parmesan cheese
½ cup chopped parsley
2 green onions, chopped
Salt, pepper to taste

Beat eggs until frothy. Add rice (cooked according to directions on package), zucchini, oil, cheese, parsley, and onions. Season to taste and bake in a casserole dish at 350 degrees for 35 to 40 minutes or until set.

WILD RICE

Serves 6–8

6 tablespoons butter
½ cup chopped parsley
½ cup chopped green onions
1 cup sliced celery
1 ½ cups washed wild rice
1 can (10 ½ ounces) condensed consommé
1 ½ cups boiling water
1 teaspoon salt
½ teaspoon marjoram or thyme
½ cup Sebastiani Chardonnay or other dry, white wine

In a heavy skillet combine butter, parsley, onions, and celery. Cook until soft, but not browned, about 10 minutes. Add rice, consommé, water, salt, and spice. Cook covered over low heat about 45 minutes. Stir lightly with fork occasionally and add a little hot water if mixture gets too dry. When rice is tender and liquid absorbed, stir in wine. Cook uncovered about 3 minutes longer, until wine is absorbed.

If you like a creamy texture, add a half can of undiluted cream of celery soup.

RISOTTO WITH MUSHROOMS

Serves 6

½ cup butter
1 medium onion, minced
1 ½ cups raw rice
1 small can sliced mushrooms, drained
⅛ teaspoon powdered saffron (optional)
½ cup Sebastiani Chardonnay or other dry, white wine
4 to 5 cups boiling chicken broth
½ cup grated Parmesan cheese
½ cup shredded Swiss cheese
Salt, white pepper to taste

Melt butter in a large, heavy skillet. Add onions and sauté very slowly, stirring frequently. Do not let them brown. Add rice, then mushrooms, and stir gently for a minute or two. Add salt and pepper to taste and stir frequently for about 10 minutes. Dissolve saffron in a tablespoon of heated wine, then add to rice with remaining wine. Add chicken broth a little at a time, stirring for 25 minutes until rice is tender and the liquid is absorbed. Stir in cheeses just before serving.

Risotto with Mushrooms, opposite page

If your family likes their sauce hot, add a small chili pepper, chopped very fine, while sauce is simmering. These peppers are very hot and a little goes a long way, so use them with caution. This recipe yields a quantity of sauce greater than you would normally use at one time. Freeze the remainder in pint jars, filling ¾ full. I always keep a supply of frozen sauce on hand—it helps put together numerous meals in a short time.

We recommend serving with a Sebastiani Zinfandel.

SPAGHETTI SAUCE

1 pound ground beef (optional)
4 tablespoons olive oil
4 tablespoons butter
4 stalks celery, chopped
4 onions, chopped
4 cloves garlic, finely chopped
¼ teaspoon thyme
¼ teaspoon rosemary
½ cup finely chopped parsley
½ cup dried Italian mushrooms, soaked in 1 cup hot water
and then chopped
1 large can solid pack tomatoes, mashed with liquid
6 cans (8 ounces each) tomato sauce
1 ½ cups water
1 cup Sebastiani Zinfandel or other dry, red wine
1 teaspoon sugar
Salt, pepper to taste

If using meat, brown meat in olive oil and butter. Add celery and onions until brown, then add garlic. Salt and pepper to taste; then add spices, mushrooms with their liquid, tomatoes, and tomato sauce. Fill tomato sauce cans with 1 ½ cups of water and add to sauce along with wine and sugar. Cook for 3 hours over low heat, stirring occasionally. If not using meat, start by browning onions and celery and proceed as above. Instead of ground beef, a piece of pot roast can be used. Brown on all sides and proceed as above, letting meat simmer in sauce. After 2 hours, remove meat from sauce and keep warm. Slice and serve as meat course for your dinner.

SPINACH DUMPLINGS

Serves 4–6

Another way to serve these spinach dumplings is to dribble 4 tablespoons melted butter over them and sprinkle generously with grated Parmesan cheese. Set under broiler until cheese melts and serve with garlic bread for a complete meal.

2 packages (10 ounces each) frozen chopped spinach or 1 ½ pounds of fresh spinach
4 tablespoons butter
2 teaspoons grated onion
¾ cup ricotta cheese
1 egg, slightly-beaten
6 tablespoons flour
¾ cup grated Parmesan cheese
6 quarts water
1 tablespoon salt
Bisquick
Spaghetti Sauce (see recipe on page 72)
Grated Parmesan cheese
Salt, pepper to taste

Cook spinach thoroughly, seasoning with salt and pepper to taste. Squeeze dry and chop finely. Melt butter in skillet over moderate heat and add spinach and onion, stirring constantly 2 to 3 minutes until most of the moisture is absorbed. Add ricotta cheese, cook 3 to 4 minutes longer, mixing well. Then remove from heat and let cool. Place cooled spinach mixture in mixing bowl and add egg, flour, cheese, and salt and pepper to taste. Mix all ingredients well, then refrigerate 45 minutes until mixture becomes quite firm. Bring water and salt to a rapid boil. Shape spinach mixture into balls and roll in Bisquick. Drop into boiling water, cooking uncovered 6 to 7 minutes until they are firm. Gently remove from water and let drain. Arrange dumplings on a platter, pour over spaghetti sauce and sprinkle with cheese.

Stuffed Artichokes, page 78

VEGETABLES

vegetable tips

1. When boiling green vegetables, such as string beans, zucchini, artichokes, sprouts, broccoli, and asparagus, bring salted water to a rolling boil. Then add 2 to 3 teaspoons of olive oil and 1 clove of garlic to the water before adding vegetables. The oil and garlic will enhance the flavor and texture of the vegetables.

2. When boiling green vegetables, leave uncovered. This will help keep the vegetables green.

3. White vegetables, such as cauliflower, onions and turnips, will stay white if pan is left uncovered while vegetables are boiling and a little lemon juice or vinegar is added to the water.

4. Do not overcook vegetables; they should be firm, not mushy.

5. Just before draining boiled green vegetables, add 1 cup of cold water and drain immediately. This will add greenness to the vegetables.

ARTICHOKE FRITTATA

Serves 6

For variations, this frittata recipe can be used with cooked asparagus, zucchini, and string beans. Simply substitute for the artichokes as indicated above. Sometimes, I make the frittata without cheese.

Serve frittata with a bottle of Sebastiani Eye of the Swan.

4 links pork sausage, skinned and cut into small pieces
½ onion, chopped
1 clove garlic, chopped
2 packages frozen artichokes or 2 cans (14 ounces each) artichokes, drained and cut into quarters lengthwise
4 eggs, well-beaten
1 teaspoon chopped parsley (optional)
¼ cup grated Parmesan cheese
Salt, pepper to taste

Sauté sausage with onion and garlic. Add artichokes and cook over low heat until tender, about 10 minutes. Season to taste with salt and pepper. Stir in eggs and turn into an oiled 8 x 8 baking dish. Sprinkle with parsley and cheese and bake at 350 degrees for 30 minutes.

ARTICHOKES WITH PORK SAUSAGE

Serves 4–6

1 or 2 packages frozen artichokes
4 to 6 links sausage, cut into 1 inch lengths
Salt, pepper to taste

Cook artichokes and sausage together in frying pan over medium heat for about 20 minutes, seasoning to taste. Keep covered when not stirring.

STUFFED ARTICHOKES

Serves 4

4 artichokes
½ cup vinegar
4 tablespoons olive oil
1 ½ cups bread crumbs
4 cloves garlic, finely chopped
4 tablespoons grated Parmesan cheese
½ teaspoon salt
1 tablespoon chopped parsley
Pepper to taste

Wash artichokes in water and vinegar to prevent discoloring. Trim bases so that artichokes can stand upright. Trim about ½ inch off points of remaining leaves. Drop artichokes into a large pot of boiling water and boil for 10 minutes. Drain and cool upside down. Then gently spread out top leaves of each artichoke and pull the tender center of thistle-like yellow leaves. Scrape out the hairy choke inside to leave the heart clean. Heat oil in a heavy skillet. Add bread crumbs, garlic, cheese, salt, parsley, and pepper. Stir well. Spoon about 2 tablespoons of stuffing into the center of each artichoke. With fingers, press rest of stuffing between the large outer leaves. Arrange artichokes close together in a deep baking dish and sprinkle 1 tablespoon olive oil over each. Pour in boiling water to a depth of 1 inch. Cover dish tightly and bake for 1 hour at 350 degrees, until tender. Serve immediately.

FRIED CARDONE (WILD ARTICHOKE)

1 or 2 stalks cardone, cut into 2 inch pieces
2 cups Bisquick
⅔ cup water
2 eggs
Olive oil
Salt, pepper to taste

Place cardone pieces in boiling, salted water for 15 to 20 minutes, taking care not to overcook. Drain well. Dip cardone into batter made by mixing Bisquick mix, water, and eggs (mixed thoroughly with a fork). Fry in deep oil and season to taste with salt and pepper.

ARTICHOKES AND PEAS

Serves 6–8

4 tablespoons olive oil
2 tablespoons butter
2 packages frozen artichokes, unthawed
1 package frozen peas, unthawed
1 clove garlic, mashed
Salt, pepper to taste

Heat oil and butter in frying pan. Add artichokes and fry slowly. After 15 minutes, add peas. Then add garlic, salt, and pepper. Cover for a few minutes and let cook over low heat. Keep turning with pancake turner until artichokes and peas are tender. Remove garlic before serving.

ARTICHOKE HEARTS

Serves 4–6

Serve with a Sebastiani Merlot.

2 tablespoons butter
4 tablespoons olive oil
12 small artichoke hearts, cut in half or 2 packages frozen hearts
½ cup Sebastiani Chardonnay or other dry, white wine
2 cloves garlic
Salt, pepper to taste

Melt butter with oil in frying pan. Add remaining ingredients and fry together 15 to 20 minutes. Fresh artichokes will take a couple of minutes longer to cook.

ASPARAGUS PARMESAN

2 pounds fresh asparagus
6 tablespoons melted butter
½ cup grated Parmesan cheese

Cut off hard ends of asparagus and peel off some of the skin. Cook asparagus in salted, boiling water for about 12 minutes. Drain the stalks and place them in a shallow baking dish. Pour over melted butter and sprinkle with Parmesan cheese (over the tips). Bake in a 400 degree oven for about 10 minutes.

EGGPLANT ITALIAN

Serves 4–6

1 small eggplant, unpeeled and cubed
1 small dry onion, chopped
6 tablespoons olive oil
1 clove garlic, minced or chopped
Dash minced chili pepper (optional)
½ cup tomato sauce
4 tablespoons grated Parmesan cheese
Salt, pepper to taste

Sauté eggplant and onion in oil, turning frequently with pancake turner. Salt and pepper to taste, then add garlic, and continue cooking until ingredients are tender, about 15 to 20 minutes. Add chili pepper and tomato sauce and stir occasionally for a few more minutes. Add cheese just prior to serving.

Try a glass of Sebastiani Pinot Noir with this dish.

EGGPLANT PARMESAN

Serves 4–6

Serve with a Sebastiani Cabernet Sauvignon.

1 ½ pounds eggplant, unpeeled and cut into ½ inch slices
Salt
Flour
¼ cup olive oil
2 cups Tomato Sauce (see recipe on page 256)
½ pound mozzarella or Monterey Jack cheese, sliced thinly
½ cup grated Parmesan cheese
2 teaspoons chopped basil

Sprinkle eggplant slices with salt and spread out on a platter. After 30 minutes, pat slices dry with paper towels. Dip each slice into flour and shake off excess. Heat oil in a heavy skillet and brown slices a few at a time. (It may be necessary to add more oil as more eggplant is browned.) After browning, transfer slices to paper towels so that they drain well. Grease a 2-quart baking dish and pour in ½ cup tomato sauce. Spread eggplant slices over sauce, top with a layer of cheese, and a sprinkling of Parmesan and basil. Top with a thin layer of tomato sauce. Repeat layers in this order until all ingredients are used, being sure to finish with a top layer of tomato sauce over the cheeses and basil. Bake for 30 minutes at 350 degrees, or until eggplant is tender when pricked with a fork.

CARROTS IN WINE

Serves 6

1 bunch carrots, sliced
Salted water
3 green onions, chopped
½ clove garlic, pressed
2 tablespoons butter
1 tablespoon flour
¼ cup canned consommé, undiluted
½ cup Sebastiani Chardonnay, or other dry, white wine
Salt, pepper to taste

Cover and steam carrots for 15 minutes in a small amount of salted water. Then drain well. In another pan, sauté onion and garlic in melted butter until golden brown. Add flour, then gradually stir in consommé and wine. Cook, stirring constantly, until thick. Add cooked carrots to sauce, then cover and reheat until bubbly. Season to taste with salt and pepper.

GOLDEN CARROT RING

Serves 12–14

5 cups grated raw carrots
4 eggs
2 cups half-and-half
1 teaspoon salt
½ teaspoon pepper
1 teaspoon sugar
1 tablespoon lemon juice
1 cup shredded almonds
Butter to grease ring mold

Cook carrots in boiling water, then drain thoroughly. Mix all other ingredients together and combine with carrots. Spread butter thoroughly over inside of 9-inch ring mold. Line with greased wax paper, then pour carrot mixture into mold and bake in 325 degree oven for 40 minutes. Turn onto a large plate and fill center with any other vegetable or mushrooms. Makes a perfect buffet dish.

CARROT LOAF

Serves 8–10

1 large bunch carrots, cut into small pieces
2 large white onions, chopped
½ pound very sharp cheddar cheese, shredded
4 eggs, beaten
Salt, white pepper to taste

Cook carrots and onions in salted, boiling water until carrots are tender. Drain thoroughly and mash. Add cheese and eggs, then salt and pepper to taste. Grease baking mold well, then pour in carrot mixture. Place mold in a shallow baking pan with water. Bake at 325 degrees for 1 hour or more. Mold is ready when it is firm when tested with a knife.

BOILED CORN

Serves 6

6 ears corn
Cold water
½ cup Sebastiani Chardonnay or other dry, white wine

Put ears of corn into large kettle of cold water, making sure all ears are covered with water. Bring to a boil and then add wine. Turn off heat and let stand 20 minutes, or until ready to serve.

BAKED EGGPLANT

⅓ to ½ cup mayonnaise
1 eggplant, cut into ½ inch slices
⅓ cup saltine crackers, crushed
⅓ cup grated Parmesan cheese

Spread mayonnaise on both sides of eggplant slices. Dip slices into a mixture of cracker crumbs and cheese. Bake on cookie sheet in 400 degree oven for 15 to 20 minutes or until eggplant is tender.

GREEN PEPPERS IN VINEGAR

Makes 1 quart

5 to 6 green bell peppers
1 teaspoon salt
3 to 4 cloves garlic
1 cup white vinegar
1 cup water
3 to 4 grape leaves

Wash bell peppers, remove seeds, and cut into quarters. Pack into a quart jar. Add salt and garlic. Boil vinegar and water together and pour over bell peppers. Add grape leaves, allowing a little vinegar to cover the leaves. Fill jar to top with vinegar and water and seal immediately. (The grape leaves keep the bell peppers firm, preventing them from getting mushy.)

FRIED MUSTARD GREENS

Mustard greens
Olive oil
1 clove garlic
Salt, pepper to taste
Kidney beans (optional)

These greens are somewhat bitter to people who haven't developed a taste for mustard greens, but once you've developed a taste for these, you'll be out every spring hunting for mustard greens.

Pick only young tender leaves of mustard greens, don't select any with yellow flowers. Wash well. Put greens in a large pot with just enough water on bottom to keep greens from sticking. Cover and cook until greens are limp. Drain and squeeze dry. Then chop. Put chopped greens into oiled frying pan with whole clove garlic and a few cooked kidney beans and fry until greens are hot.

STEAMED MUSTARD GREENS

Mustard greens
Olive oil
1 clove garlic
Salt, pepper to taste

Place clean greens in oiled pan. Simmer, covered, over low fire and stir occasionally until tender. Serve hot and season to taste.

STUFFED PEPPERS

Serves 4

4 medium bell peppers
1 onion, chopped
2 tablespoons butter
1 cup cooked rice
1 ½ cups cooked meat, ground
½ cup grated Parmesan cheese
1 pound canned tomatoes with liquid, mashed
½ cup Sebastiani Zinfandel or Cabernet Sauvignon, or other dry, red wine
Salt, pepper to taste

Cut stems, remove seeds and veins from bell peppers. Cook in rapidly boiling salted water, uncovered, for 5 minutes. Remove and turn upside down to drain well. Sauté onion lightly in butter. Add rice and meat, along with cheese. Season to taste with salt and pepper. Mix well and stuff mixture into peppers. Place in a deep casserole and surround with tomatoes and wine. Bake 45 minutes to 1 hour at 350 degrees, basting bell peppers occasionally. Spoon tomatoes over bell peppers before serving.

Sebastiani Cabernet Sauvignon will match well with these stuffed peppers.

Peas with Prosciutto, opposite page

PEAS WITH PROSCIUTTO

Serves 4–6

Perfect with a vibrant Sebastiani Zinfandel on the table.

2 tablespoons butter
4 tablespoons finely chopped onion
2 slices bacon or prosciutto, cut into 1 inch strips
1 clove garlic, pressed
¼ cup Sebastiani Chardonnay or other, dry, white wine
2 packages (10 ounces each) frozen peas
Salt, pepper to taste

Melt butter in skillet and add onions and bacon or prosciutto. Cook, stirring frequently, until onions are soft, not brown. Add garlic, then wine. Add peas and let simmer 15 minutes over low heat until peas are tender. Salt and pepper to taste before serving.

GRATED POTATOES

Serves 6

3 medium-sized potatoes
1 teaspoon olive oil
2 tablespoons butter
Salt, pepper to taste

Pare, wash, and grate potatoes on a medium grater. Spread them in a skillet that has been well-greased with oil and butter. Cook potatoes on medium heat, covered, until bottom is brown. Season with salt and pepper. With a pancake turner, reverse and brown the other side. Season again and serve hot from the pan.

GREEN POTATOES

Serves 8–10

6 large potatoes
¾ cup light cream
1 teaspoon sugar
½ cup butter
2 teaspoons salt
¼ teaspoon pepper
1 package frozen chopped spinach, cooked and drained

Boil potatoes with their skins on. Peel and mash. Add cream, sugar, butter, salt, and pepper. Chop spinach finely and add to potato mixture. Beat all together until well-blended. Bake in 400 degree oven for 20 to 30 minutes until potatoes are thoroughly heated.

POTATO SLICES IN ONION BUTTER

Serves 8–10

½ cup melted butter
½ package onion soup mix
1 teaspoon salt
½ cup water
4 or 5 medium-sized potatoes, unpeeled and sliced
Pepper to taste

In a mixing bowl, combine butter, soup mix, salt, and pepper. Pour water into a 2-quart casserole dish. Arrange a layer of potato slices in casserole, then spread a tablespoonful of onion mixture over top. Repeat, making five layers. Cover and bake 45 minutes to 1 hour at 350 degrees.

This recipe can be prepared ahead of time and refrigerated until ready to use. Allow 5 to 10 minutes longer baking time if potatoes are refrigerated before baking.

SCALLOPED POTATOES AND ONIONS

Serves 6–8

For an interesting variation, substitute condensed mushroom soup for the flour and milk.

This dish is wonderful with a Sebastiani Zinfandel.

4 cups potatoes, pared and sliced thin
1 onion, peeled and sliced thin
3 tablespoons butter
1 ½ teaspoons salt
White pepper to taste
3 tablespoons flour
1 ½ cups milk

Grease a baking dish, preferably with butter. Place potato slices in dish in layers and sprinkle with onion, salt, pepper, and flour. Dot with butter, then pour milk over all. Bake in a 325 degree oven for 1 ½ hours. A foil cover may be used the first ½ hour if desired. If so, cooking time will be reduced.

LEFTOVER MASHED POTATO PANCAKES

Here is an excellent use for cold mashed potatoes. This dish is a good complement to any dinner.

1 to 2 cups cold mashed potatoes
1 or 2 beaten eggs
2 or 3 tablespoons flour
Salt, pepper to taste
3 or 4 tablespoons butter

Add egg, flour, salt, and pepper to potatoes and shape into little pancakes. Fry in butter and turn once after browned on one side.

LEFTOVER POTATOES WITH TOMATO SAUCE

1 clove garlic, chopped
1 tablespoon chopped parsley
2 tablespoons butter
¼ to ½ cup tomato sauce
Leftover mashed potatoes

Sauté garlic and parsley lightly in butter. Add tomato sauce (this amount determined by the amount of potatoes). Add potatoes and stir well with fork over low heat until hot.

STUFFED POTATOES

Serves 10

5 potatoes
1 cup cottage cheese and chives
1 cube butter
1 egg
2 tablespoons mayonnaise
½ teaspoon Accent
Salt, pepper, garlic salt to taste
Paprika

Bake potatoes until thoroughly cooked. Cut each potato in half and scoop out the insides. Reserve potato skins. Using an electric mixer, mix potato insides with cottage cheese and chives, butter, and remaining ingredients. Beat until all ingredients are thoroughly blended, season to taste. Re-stuff the potato skins with this mixture, sprinkle with paprika, and bake in a 450 degree oven for 15 minutes.

CREAMED SPINACH AND MUSHROOMS

Serves 6–8

2 tablespoons chopped green onions
2 tablespoons butter
¼ cup flour
1 teaspoon salt
Dash of pepper
1 ½ cups light cream
½ cup Sebastiani Chardonnay, or other dry, white wine
2 cups cooked chopped spinach
½ cup cooked mushrooms

Cook onions lightly in butter; stir in flour, salt, and pepper. Slowly stir in cream; cook and stir until mixture boils and thickens. Add wine and cook a few minutes longer. Cook spinach, drain well, and squeeze dry. Add spinach and mushrooms to cream sauce and heat well.

SPINACH ALMONDINE

Serves 6–8

2 packages frozen chopped spinach
1 can cream of mushroom soup
2 tablespoons butter
Pinch of ground mace
½ cup blanched and slivered almonds, browned in butter

Thaw and drain spinach well. Place in a casserole dish and add remaining ingredients. Sprinkle a few almonds on top and cook in a 375 degree oven for 45 minutes.

SPINACH LOAF

Serves 4

5 tablespoons butter
½ onion, grated
5 level tablespoons flour
1 ½ cups milk
3 eggs, separated
1 clove garlic, pressed
¼ cup grated Parmesan cheese
½ teaspoon white pepper
½ teaspoon salt
½ cup chopped mushrooms, drained (optional)
2 packages frozen spinach, cooked, drained, and finely chopped

In top of double boiler, melt butter and add onion. Gradually add flour and milk, stirring constantly. Cook until thick, then remove from heat. Beat egg yolks in a mixing bowl, then gradually stir in onion-milk mixture. Add garlic, cheese, white pepper, salt, and mushrooms. Let cool. Beat egg whites and fold into mixture along with spinach. Turn into a loaf pan or casserole dish and bake at 350 degrees 30 to 35 minutes until firm.

This dish can also be baked in a mold. Grease the mold well, then line with wax paper that has also been greased. Pour the mixture into the mold and place mold in a pan. Add enough simmering water to reach about ¾ way up the sides of the mold. Bake in the middle shelf of oven, making sure that temperature is regulated, so that water is kept at a very low simmer.

SHERRY-GLAZED YAMS

Serves 6

3 large or 6 medium yams
1 cup dry sherry or cream sherry
1 teaspoon grated orange rind
½ cup sugar
½ cup brown sugar
4 tablespoons butter

Parboil yams in their jackets. When tender, drain, peel, and cut each yam into 4 to 6 pieces. Place in a buttered, shallow baking dish. Combine remaining ingredients and cook over low heat, stirring constantly, until thick. Pour mixture over yams. Bake uncovered at 350 degrees for 25 minutes.

SWISS CHARD

Serves 4–6

2 bundles Swiss Chard, greens only
2 tablespoons butter
2 tablespoons olive oil
1 clove garlic
Salt, pepper to taste

Boil Swiss chard in salted water until not quite tender. Heat butter and oil in frying pan and add garlic. Add well-drained chard and simmer for 15 minutes. Season to taste with salt and pepper and remove garlic before serving.

ZUCCHINI AND EGGS

Serves 6

2 tablespoons butter
4 tablespoons oil
4 or 5 small zucchini, cut into pieces
½ onion, chopped
2 eggs
Grated Parmesan cheese
Salt, pepper, garlic salt to taste

Melt butter and oil. Sauté zucchini and onion together, seasoning to taste. Break in eggs and stir, mixing well. As soon as eggs are cooked, remove from heat, top with cheese, and serve immediately.

The white stalks of the Swiss chard can be prepared in this same manner, but they require a longer cooking time. If desired, steam the stalks with butter and sprinkle with Parmesan cheese before serving.

A Sebastiani Pinot Noir is ideal with this dish.

FRIED ZUCCHINI

Serves 4

2 tablespoons butter
2 tablespoons olive oil
½ onion, chopped
¼ teaspoon garlic salt
¼ teaspoon salt
⅛ teaspoon pepper
4 medium zucchini, unpeeled and sliced or cubed

Melt butter and oil in frying pan. Add onion and seasonings and sauté until golden brown, stirring frequently. Add zucchini and turn occasionally with pancake turner until tender.

ZUCCHINI LOAF

Serves 4

4 or 5 medium-sized zucchini
4 tablespoons chopped green onion
4 tablespoons grated Parmesan cheese
⅓ cup cracker crumbs
4 eggs, beaten
⅓ cup chopped parsley (optional)
Salt, pepper, garlic salt to taste

Cut zucchini into 1 inch rounds and boil for 20 minutes. Drain well, place in saucepan, and mash. Add onions, cheese, crackers, and seasonings. Add eggs and mix well. Turn into greased loaf pan and bake at 350 degrees for 30 minutes. This can also be served cold, cut into cubes.

ZUCCHINI PANCAKES

Serves 6–8

2 cups buttermilk pancake mix
⅔ cup water
2 eggs
2 tablespoons grated Parmesan cheese
2 large zucchini, unpeeled and shredded
Oil
Butter
Salt, pepper to taste

Make batter with pancake mix, water, eggs, cheese, and salt and pepper to taste. Put shredded zucchini into batter and mix well. Spoon out with a large spoon and fry in oil and butter over medium heat. Turn when brown.

ZUCCHINI STUFFED WITH CHEESE

Serves 6–8

6 medium-sized zucchini, whole and unpeeled
8 ounces sharp Tillamook cheese
Salt, pepper to taste

Cook zucchini in boiling, salted water until tender, but firm, about 10 to 15 minutes. Drain and cut into halves. Remove seeds with a thin knife and sprinkle with salt and pepper. Cut cheese to size necessary to fill the zucchini and bake in a 350 degree oven for 20 minutes.

If batter is allowed to stand, it will thicken and it will be necessary to add more water. When in season, zucchini flowers can be prepared in this manner. Be sure to remove the pistil from the flowers first and handle them gently while dipping into the batter as they are fragile. This batter recipe can also be used with any other cooked vegetables, e.g., cauliflower, celery, broccoli, and artichokes. Other variations include adding pre-cooked mushrooms, 1 pressed clove garlic, ½ cup parsley, or 1 small container sour cream to the batter before using, and reduce the amount of water to ½ cup.

ZUCCHINI FRITTERS

Serves 4

1 to 2 zucchini, unpeeled
1 cup cold water
1 ½ cups Bisquick
1 egg
1 tablespoon grated Parmesan cheese
Olive oil
Salt, pepper, garlic salt to taste

Slice zucchini into long, thin ovals. Add water to pancake mix, beating with a fork. Add egg and continue beating until smooth. Add cheese and seasonings to taste. Dip zucchini into this batter and fry on both sides in deep oil. Sprinkle a little more salt on top and serve at once.

STUFFED ZUCCHINI

Serves 4–6

4 medium zucchini, unpeeled
2 tablespoons olive oil
1 tablespoon butter
½ cup finely chopped onions
4 links sausage, finely chopped (optional)
1 clove garlic, pressed
1 egg, lightly beaten
2 ounces prosciutto, finely chopped (optional)
½ cup fresh bread crumbs
6 tablespoons grated Parmesan cheese
½ teaspoon oregano
Salt, pepper to taste

Boil zucchini for about 10 minutes, then cut in half lengthwise, and scoop out most of the pulp. Set shells aside and chop pulp. Heat oil and butter in a heavy skillet and cook onions and sausage. Add zucchini pulp and garlic and cook for about 5 minutes, stirring frequently. Pour into a large sieve and let drain. Into zucchini mixture, beat the egg, prosciutto, bread crumbs, 2 teaspoons cheese, oregano, and salt and pepper to taste. Spoon this into hollowed zucchini shells, mounding tops slightly. Place into an oiled shallow baking dish, sprinkle with remaining cheese, and dribble a few drops of olive oil over each shell. Cover dish tightly with foil and bake for 30 minutes at 375 degrees. Remove foil and bake another 10 minutes.

FISH

Baked Fish, page 108

BACCALA

Serves 4

1 pound salted codfish
1 or 2 dried onions, finely chopped
6 tablespoons olive oil
1 tablespoon chopped parsley
¼ teaspoon pepper
1 ½ tablespoons flour
1 ¼ cups milk

Soak fish in cold water for 8 hours, changing water several times. Place fish in cold water (enough to cover) and bring to a boil. Drain and place on baking dish. Sauté onions in oil. When soft, add parsley, pepper, and flour and blend well. Pour mixture over fish, then add milk, and stir liquid together. Bake fish at least 1 hour in 275 degree oven.

If desired, this recipe can be prepared with tomato sauce. Substitute 1 can (8 ounces) tomato sauce for the milk and eliminate flour.

CALAMARI (SQUID) IN TOMATO SAUCE

Serves 4–6

2 tablespoons oil
4 tablespoons butter
1/2 onion, chopped
2 cloves garlic, chopped
1 tablespoon chopped parsley
1 can (8 ounces) tomato sauce
1/4 cup Sebastiani Chardonnay, or other dry, white wine
1 pound squid, body cut into 1 inch pieces and leave heads whole
Salt, pepper to taste

Melt oil and butter in frying pan and sauté onions lightly, seasoning to taste with salt and pepper. Add garlic and parsley and sauté for 1 minute. Add tomato sauce and wine. Cover and simmer 15 to 20 minutes. Then add fish and cook for an additional 12 to 15 minutes. Take care not to overcook as fish will become tough. Serve at once.

CALAMARI (SQUID) IN WINE

Serves 4–6

This dish is nicely complemented by a Sebastiani Chardonnay.

1 pound squid, body cut into 1 inch pieces and leave heads whole
2 tablespoons oil
4 tablespoons butter
1 clove garlic, pressed
1 tablespoon chopped parsley
1 cup Sebastiani Chardonnay, or other dry, white wine
Salt, pepper to taste

Lightly brown squid in oil and butter in frying pan, seasoning to taste with salt and pepper. Add garlic and parsley and sauté briefly. Then add wine, stir once, and cover and simmer 12 to 15 minutes.

BAKED CLAMS

Serves 6–8

1 large onion, finely chopped
4 tablespoons finely chopped parsley
2 tablespoons olive oil
2 tablespoons butter
1 pound clams, chopped
2 slices bacon, fried crisp and chopped
5 to 6 slices bread, soaked in milk and squeezed dry
1 can (8 ounces) tomato sauce
1/2 cup buttered soda cracker crumbs
1/2 cup grated Parmesan cheese
Salt, pepper to taste

Brown onion and parsley in oil and butter. Add clams, bacon, and bread. Salt and pepper to taste, then add tomato sauce. Bake in ramekins or clam shells, topping each with a sprinkling of cracker crumbs. Bake 30 minutes at 350 degrees. Sprinkle with cheese before serving.

CRACKED CRAB

2 cooked crabs
Juice of 6 lemons
1 or 2 ounces vinegar
1 or 2 ounces olive oil
Dash of paprika
Dash of pepper
Few drops of Tabasco sauce
Few drops of Worcestershire sauce

Break off claws from crab and crack with nutcracker. Pull off backs and remove all spongy parts below. Pull off small piece of shell on underside of crab and remove fat. Set aside. Cut body of each crab into 6 pieces.

Combine crab fat with remaining ingredients and pour mixture over crab meat and crab legs. Marinate several hours or overnight, turning occasionally. Serve with French bread, large towel bibs, and a Sebastiani dry white wine.

EASY DEVILED CRAB

Serves 4

3 tablespoons butter or margarine
2 tablespoons flour
1 cup milk, heated
1 teaspoon salt
Dash cayenne pepper
1 teaspoon Worcestershire sauce
2 egg yolks, slightly beaten
2 cups crabmeat, fresh, frozen, or canned
1/2 teaspoon lemon juice
1/4 cup Sebastiani Chardonnay, or other dry, white wine
4 individual baking shells
2/3 cup buttered bread crumbs
4 lemon slices
Paprika

Recipe continued on following page

Melt butter; stir in flour and milk. Season with salt, cayenne, and Worcestershire. Cook, stirring constantly, until thick. Add egg yolks and crab while stirring. Cook 3 minutes and stir in lemon juice and wine. Spoon mixture into individual baking shells or ramekins and cover with buttered crumbs. Top with a lemon slice and a sprinkling of paprika. Bake in a 450 degree oven about 20 to 25 minutes until brown.

CRAB OR SHRIMP SOUFFLÉ

Serves 6–8

4 slices white bread
1 can crab or shrimp
1/2 cup mayonnaise
1/2 cup chopped green onions, tops only
1/2 cup finely chopped parsley
1 small can water chestnuts, sliced
1 small can mushrooms
2 eggs
1 1/4 cups milk
1/2 cup Sebastiani Chardonnay, or other dry, white wine
1/2 cup cream of mushroom soup
1/2 cup grated Parmesan cheese

Grease a deep casserole dish. Dice 2 slices of bread and place in bottom. Mix fish, mayonnaise, onions, parsley, water chestnuts, and mushrooms. Spread over bread cubes, then lay 2 slices of bread over this. Beat eggs into milk and wine and pour over entire casserole. Let stand in refrigerator overnight, covered. Bake 20 minutes at 325 degrees. Spread top with mushroom soup and cheese, then bake for an additional hour.

When fresh crab is in season, I use a double amount (2 cups) in this recipe.

We recommend serving Sebastiani Eye of the Swan with this dish.

Sebastiani Symphony nicely complements the flavors of this dish.

BAKED FISH SLICES

4 to 6 slices cod, halibut, or sole
1/3 to 1/2 cup mayonnaise
1/3 cup cracker meal
Salt, pepper to taste

Season fish slices with salt and pepper. Spread mayonnaise on both sides of slices and dip into cracker meal. Bake in 400 degree oven on cookie sheet for 20 to 30 minutes, or until fish is tender. Cooking time will depend upon the thickness of the slices.

STEAMED CLAMS

Serves 4

4 tablespoons butter
2 cloves garlic, finely chopped
2 tablespoons chopped parsley
1/2 cup water
3 dozen clams, well-cleaned
Dash or two of pepper

Melt butter in pot; add garlic, parsley, and pepper and stir until well-blended. Add water and clams and cover pot. Let steam over low heat, shaking pot occasionally, until shells open, about 15 to 20 minutes. Serve clams in their shells in soup plates and pour broth over them, or broth can be served separately in a cup.

If raw crab is used, add to cioppino along with the other raw fish and cook as usual, keeping crab on the bottom of the pot. There are many variations to this dish: any type of shellfish (e.g., lobster or mussels) can be used. Bass may also be added if you wish. When serving this dish, fingers are the best utensils to use since the crab, prawns, and clams are still in their shells. Each guest would appreciate a dish towel to help him along while he enjoys this dish. We serve a mixed green salad, a Sebastiani dry white wine, and lots of French bread along with cioppino for a complete meal.

CIOPPINO

Serves 4–6

1 large cooked crab (about 2 to 3 pounds)
½ cup olive oil
½ small white onion, chopped
1 large clove garlic, chopped
2 tablespoons chopped parsley
1 cup Sebastiani Chardonnay, or other dry, white wine
1 can (8 ounces) tomato sauce
Dash cayenne pepper
1 tablespoon finely chopped dry Italian mushrooms (optional)
¼ teaspoon salt
⅛ teaspoon pepper
1 pound ling cod, cut in large chunks
½ pound frozen or fresh prawns
1 ½ pounds clams in shells

Crack crab legs, but leave whole. Crack shell, take out meat, and cut into large chunks. Retain fat from the wings of the shell. Add oil and brown onion and garlic in large pot over medium heat. Add parsley and fat of crab. Mix well, then add wine, tomato sauce, seasonings, and mushrooms. Cover and simmer over low heat for 20 to 30 minutes. Add fish, prawns, and clams. Let cook over low heat for 20 minutes. Do not stir; simply shake the pot occasionally. Add crab and heat just until crab becomes hot. Take care not to stir. Serve immediately.

FILET OF SOLE WITH GRAPES

Serves 4

¼ cup butter
1 pound small filets of sole
½ teaspoon salt
1 tablespoon lemon juice
Sprinkle of cayenne pepper
½ cup Sebastiani Chardonnay, or other dry, white wine
½ cup halved white seedless grapes
½ teaspoon grated fresh lemon peel
1 teaspoon chervil

Melt butter in heavy frying pan; add filets and cook for about 5 minutes until slightly browned. Turn carefully with a spatula, sprinkling with salt, lemon juice, and cayenne. Pour wine over fish and continue cooking until done, about 5 minutes. With a spatula, gently lift fish onto heated serving plates or platter. Add grapes, lemon peel, and chervil to the sauce left in the pan. Bring sauce to a boil and simmer until the grapes are heated through. Pour over the filets and serve at once.

FRIED OYSTERS

Serves 4–6

2 dozen medium oysters
2 eggs
½ package cracker crumbs
4 tablespoons olive oil
2 tablespoons butter
Salt, pepper, garlic salt to taste
Lemon wedges

Wash oysters well, rinse, and dry thoroughly. Beat eggs, then dip oysters in egg. Roll in cracker crumbs and fry in oil and butter. Season to taste. Serve with lemon wedges.

BAKED FISH

Serves 6–8

A Sebastiani Chardonnay is a perfect complement to this fish.

1 onion, chopped
4 tablespoons oil
6 tablespoons butter
1 large can solid packed tomatoes, mashed and undrained
2 potatoes, peeled and sliced thinly
1 striped bass (about 3 to 5 pounds)
2 to 3 teaspoons chopped parsley
2 cloves garlic
¾ cup Sebastiani Chardonnay, or other dry, white wine
1 lemon, sliced thinly
Salt, pepper, garlic salt to taste

Sauté onion in oil and 2 tablespoons butter, adding salt, pepper, and garlic salt to taste. Add tomatoes with their liquid; then add potatoes and cook until potatoes are almost tender. Meanwhile prepare fish. Cut slits across width of fish every 2 inches on both sides and season generously with salt, pepper, and garlic salt. Mix and chop together parsley and garlic, then rub in slits and inside fish. Place in shallow oiled baking dish. Cut 4 tablespoons butter into pieces and place on top of fish. Bake at 350 degrees a few minutes until butter is melted and slightly brown. Pour wine over fish, then pour over the tomato-potato mixture. Lay lemon slices on top of fish and cook until fish is done (about 45 minutes), shaking pan slightly a few times and basting occasionally. If fish sticks to pan, it can easily be lifted out with 2 pancake turners, using one at each end of the fish. Place on platter, pour sauce over, and serve.

RICE AND CLAMS

Serves 6

Be sure to wash the clams well to remove all the sand. When serving, place soup bowls on the dinner table for empty clam shells and have plenty of napkins on hand as fingers are a must for eating clams.

1 onion, chopped
2 tablespoons oil
6 to 8 tablespoons butter
4 cloves garlic, pressed
2 tablespoons chopped parsley
1 sprig thyme, chopped or ¼ teaspoon dry thyme
¼ cup dry Italian mushrooms, cut into pieces
1 can (8 ounces) tomato sauce
⅔ cup Sebastiani Chardonnay, or other dry, white wine
4 cups water
2 cups uncooked rice
3 dozen clams (in shells)
Grated Parmesan cheese
Salt, pepper to taste

Sauté onion in oil and butter over low heat. Sprinkle generously with salt and pepper and stir frequently. Add garlic, parsley, thyme, and stir. Add mushrooms, tomato sauce, wine, and water. Cover and simmer for 20 minutes. Add rice and mix together well. Add more water if necessary and a dash of salt. Stir frequently to prevent rice from sticking and cook uncovered until rice is almost cooked, about 20 minutes. Salt to taste at this point. Add clams and stir. Cover again and let steam on slow fire until clams have opened. Stir occasionally and serve with cheese.

FILETS FLORENTINE

Serves 4

2 pounds spinach or 2 packages frozen spinach, chopped
4 tablespoons butter
½ cup water
½ cup Sebastiani Chardonnay, or other dry, white wine
3 peppercorns
1 small onion
1 sprig parsley
4 fish filets
2 tablespoons flour
½ cup heavy cream
Few grains nutmeg
Few drops lemon juice
Grated Parmesan cheese
Salt, pepper to taste

Cook spinach, drain well, and chop finely. Season to taste with 2 tablespoons butter, salt, and pepper. Arrange on a well-buttered oval baking dish and keep warm. Combine water with wine, peppercorns, onion, parsley, and more salt and pepper to taste. Bring to a boil and let cook 5 minutes. Add fish and simmer until fish is cooked through, about 5 minutes longer. Remove fish to a hot plate; let liquid simmer 2 to 3 minutes longer and strain. Melt 2 tablespoons butter in a separate saucepan and blend well with flour. Stirring constantly, gradually add strained broth from the fish. Continue stirring until thick. Add cream, nutmeg, and lemon juice. Place cooked fish filets on bed of spinach, cover with wine sauce, and sprinkle liberally with cheese. Place dish in 450 degree oven for 5 minutes until cheese is delicately browned.

STUFFED FILETS OF SOLE

Serves 8

Serve with a Sebastiani Chardonnay.

½ teaspoon minced onion
I teaspoon minced celery
I tablespoon butter or oil
½ cup bread crumbs
I egg
I small can shrimp, chopped
8 medium filets of sole
½ cup milk
1 can cream of mushroom soup
½ pound fresh crab meat or I small can
Paprika
Salt, and white pepper to taste

Sauté onion and celery lightly in butter or oil. Add bread crumbs, salt, and other seasoning, if desired. Cool; add egg and shrimp. Place 1 tablespoon of this mixture on each filet and roll. Fasten with toothpick and place fish in baking dish. Mix milk with soup and half the crab. Pour over filets and top with remaining crab. Sprinkle with paprika. Bake in 325 degree oven for 30 minutes.

MEATS

Saltimbocca, page 127

meat tips

1. In meat dishes that call for wine, always heat wine first before adding. If cold wine is used, it tends to make the meat tough.

2. When oil is called for in a recipe, a good grade of olive oil should be used.

3. It's better not to buy ready-ground hamburger. There is a high percentage of fat and gristle in this meat which is rapidly cooked away and leaves very little actual meat. Buy ground round or chuck if you can.

4. Always trim off excess fat from meats.

5. Fresh herbs have more flavor than dry herbs and should be used at all times if available. This is especially true when cooking meats and you will find your meats have a much better flavor cooked with fresh herbs. Perhaps you could grow your own herbs in a window box or garden.

6. If you do buy prepared herbs, be sure to choose chopped herbs and not the powdered type.

Accompany with a Sebastiani
Cabernet Sauvignon.

BOILED BEEF

Serves 6

1 boneless rump roast or chuck roast (about 2 to 2 ½ pounds), trimmed of fat
1 tablespoon salt
2 onions
2 carrots
2 stalks celery
4 to 5 sprigs parsley
3 to 4 peppercorns
2 cloves garlic

Place meat in a soup pot and add enough cold water to cover completely.
Add salt, bring to a boil over high heat, skimming surface when foam rises.
Reduce heat and partially cover. Cook for 1 hour. Add vegetables, peppercorns,
and garlic and cook 1 hour longer or until meat is tender. Remove meat to
carving board and cut into slices. Arrange on platter and surround with carrots
and onions. Strain broth and serve as soup with a fine pasta in it.

SHORT RIBS OF BEEF

4 tablespoons oil
2 tablespoons butter
4 short ribs
Salt, pepper, garlic salt to taste
1 onion, chopped
1 can (18 ounces) solid pack tomatoes with liquid
½ cup Sebastiani Cabernet Sauvignon or other dry, red wine
1 teaspoon paprika

In a deep casserole dish, add oil, butter, and short ribs well-seasoned with salt,
pepper, and garlic salt. Turn ribs so that they brown well on all sides. Add onion
and stir until slightly brown. Then add tomatoes, wine, and paprika.

Cover and place in 325 degree oven. Cook 2 to 3 hours until short ribs are tender
when tested with a fork. Turn 2 to 3 times while baking. If short ribs seem dry,
add a little water during cooking.

CORNED BEEF AND CABBAGE

Sebastiani Merlot serves as a fine accompaniment to this dish.

1 package corned beef
2 bay leaves
3 to 4 peppercorns
1 clove garlic
3 onions
2 to 3 peeled potatoes, cut in half
3 carrots (optional)
1 head cabbage, cut into wedges

In a deep saucepan, place the corned beef and add enough water to cover. Add bay leaves, peppercorns, and garlic and simmer according to direction given on the package of corned beef. Add onions, potatoes, and carrots half an hour before cooking time is completed and add cabbage for the last 15 minutes of cooking. Serve the beef surrounded by the vegetables and use mustard as a condiment.

EASY CHUCK ROAST

Serve a Sebastiani Merlot with this meat dish.

4 tablespoons oil
2 tablespoons butter
1 chuck roast
Salt, pepper, and garlic powder to taste
1 can mushroom soup, undiluted
1 can onion soup, undiluted
1 cup Sebastiani Zinfandel, or other dry, red wine

Melt oil and butter in Dutch oven on top of stove. Brown roast well on both sides, seasoning well with salt, pepper, and garlic powder. Mix together soups and wine, add to roast and cover. Bake at 350 degrees for 2 ½ hours. Turn at least 2 or 3 times while baking.

BRAINS AND EGGS

Serves 4

2 sets calf brains
4 or 5 eggs
Salt, pepper to taste

Remove membranes from outsides of brains and wash thoroughly. Put brains in boiling water for 15 minutes. Remove and cut into 1 inch chunks. Mix brains with eggs that have been seasoned with salt and pepper. Fry as you would scrambled eggs.

CALF BRAINS

Serves 4

2 sets calf brains
1 egg
½ cup cracker meal
Salt, pepper to taste
Lemon wedges

Remove membranes from outsides of brains and wash thoroughly. Drain or pat dry with a paper towel. Beat egg with a fork and roll brains in egg and then in the cracker meal that has been mixed with salt and pepper. In a well-greased pan, bake at 350 degrees, turning when brown, and cook for a total of 25 minutes. Serve with lemon wedges.

FLAMING HAM

Serves 10–12

1 ham (about 6 to 7 pounds)
1 ⅓ cups brown sugar
2 tablespoons flour
½ teaspoon ground cloves
2 tablespoons water
2 tablespoons orange extract
½ cup warm brandy

Bake ham, following directions on package. Mix 1 cup sugar, flour, and cloves moistened with water. Use this as a glaze during the last 30 minutes of baking. When ham is done, transfer to a platter and pat on remaining brown sugar, mixed with orange extract. Carry ham to table and ignite. Then spoon over warm brandy to extend the flaming time.

HAM LOAF

Serves 6

1 pound uncooked ham, ground
½ pound lean ground pork
1 egg, slightly beaten
½ cup milk
½ cup cracker or bread crumbs
½ teaspoon paprika
½ teaspoon salt
½ onion, grated
½ cup tomato soup

Combine ham and pork. Mix together egg, milk, crumbs, and remaining ingredients. Add to meat and blend well. Bake in 350 degree oven 45 to 50 minutes. Top with sauce before serving (recipe on next page).

HAM LOAF SAUCE

1 tablespoon butter
1 tablespoon flour
¼ cup sugar
1 teaspoon dry mustard
¼ cup vinegar
1 ½ cups tomato juice
1 egg, slightly beaten

Melt butter; add flour and stir well. Add remaining ingredients, the egg last, and cook until thick. Serve with Ham Loaf on previous page.

GLAZED HAM

Serves 6–8

This glazed ham pairs well with a Sebastiani Pinot Noir.

1 canned ham (about 3 to 4 pounds)
1 ½ cups Sebastiani Chardonnay, or other dry, white wine
½ cup brown sugar

Place ham in shallow baking pan; pour over 1 cup wine and bake 1 hour at 325 degrees. Combine brown sugar with remaining wine. Cook, stirring constantly, until thick. Baste ham occasionally with this mixture during and additional half hour of cooking. You may need to add a little water while baking if the pan gets dry.

BOILED ITALIAN SAUSAGE AND POTATOES

4 Italian sausages
2 medium potatoes, cut in half
Olive oil
Vinegar
Salt, pepper to taste

Prick skins of sausages with a fork in several places. Place sausage along with potatoes in skillet and cover with boiling water. Cook until potatoes are tender, about 20 to 30 minutes. Drain well and cut sausage into 1 ½ inch pieces. Cut potatoes into smaller pieces and marinate with oil and vinegar, adding salt and pepper to taste. Serve hot.

SYMPHONY HAM

Try a medium-bodied Sebastiani Pinot Noir with this dish.

1 canned ham (about 7 to 8 pounds)
3 cups Sebastiani Symphony or other sweet, white wine
Maple syrup for basting

Marinate ham in wine for 8 hours, turning frequently. Bake in a 300 degree oven for 1 hour, basting often with wine. After 1 hour, score top of ham and brush well with maple syrup. Bake ham for 30 minutes longer; slice as thinly as possible and serve.

JOE'S SPECIAL – FROM MARIN JOE'S RESTAURANT

Serves 4–5 with generous helpings

If available, a link of Italian sausage adds zest to this dish. Simply break it up into very small pieces and add it to the beef prior to browning.

Enjoy with a Sebastiani dry red wine.

1 small onion, chopped
2 tablespoons oil
1 tablespoon butter
1 pound ground beef
Salt, pepper, garlic salt to taste
1 clove garlic, pressed
¼ cup Sebastiani Chardonnay, or other dry, white wine
1 package frozen spinach, chopped
3 tablespoons grated Parmesan cheese
1 can (4 ounces) sliced mushrooms, drained (optional)
2 eggs

Sauté onion slightly with oil and butter; add ground beef. Sprinkle salt, pepper, and garlic salt over meat while browning, then add garlic and sauté lightly. Add wine. Add spinach, stirring frequently until thawed out and cooked. Blend cheese in well, then add mushrooms. Mix in eggs a few minutes before serving.

ROAST LAMB SHANKS

Serves 2

2 lamb shanks
2 bell peppers
2 white onions
1 medium-sized potato, cut into quarters
½ teaspoon thyme
½ cup Sebastiani Chardonnay, or other dry, white wine
Salt, pepper, garlic salt to taste

Season shanks generously with salt, pepper, and garlic salt. Halve bell peppers and onions and place in a greased roasting pan along with the shanks and potato pieces. Season to taste. Bake at 350 degrees for 1 ½ hours. Add wine when meat has browned and is nearly done. If meat becomes cooked before potato pieces, remove meat from pan and wrap in foil to keep warm. Add meat to rest of mixture before serving.

ROAST LEG OF LAMB

1 lemon
1 leg of lamb
2 cloves garlic, pressed
¼ cup olive oil
½ cup Sebastiani Chardonnay, or other dry, white wine
3 to 4 potatoes, quartered
4 green bell peppers, left whole or cut in half
6 small onions
6 carrots, cut in half (optional)
Salt, pepper to taste

Cut lemon in half and rub the lamb with the juice. Salt and pepper generously and spread garlic on all sides. Put lamb into large shallow roasting pan with oil and wine. Bake at 325 degrees, basting occasionally. After 1 hour, add potatoes, bell peppers, onions, and carrots, season with salt and pepper. Add more oil if necessary to prevent drying. Turn vegetables gently while cooking; if potatoes cook before other vegetables, remove and keep hot. Total cooking time 2½ hours.

The elegant flavors in the Sebastiani Cabernet Sauvignon complement the lamb shanks nicely.

Serve with a Sebastiani Zinfandel or Barbera.

Roast Leg of Lamb, opposite page

KIDNEYS

Serves 4–6

6 lamb or 4 veal kidneys
Salted water
2 tablespoons vinegar
2 tablespoons olive oil
½ onion, chopped
1 clove garlic, chopped
½ teaspoon chopped parsley
¼ cup Sebastiani Chardonnay or other dry, white wine
Salt, pepper to taste

Plunge kidneys in boiling water. Remove skins and soak in cold salted water to which vinegar has been added for 30 minutes. Slice kidneys thin, removing tubes and tissues and season with salt and pepper. Heat oil in a frying pan and add onion, garlic, and parsley, sautéing lightly for 2 minutes. Then add kidneys and fry over high heat for a few minutes. Do not overcook as it makes kidneys tough. Add hot wine, stir once, and serve immediately.

BAKED SPARERIBS

A Sebastiani Zinfandel is ideal with this full-flavored meat.

1 side spareribs (about 2 pounds)
Garlic salt
Soy sauce
Paprika
Salt, pepper to taste

Cut spareribs into small pieces and sprinkle on both sides with remaining ingredients. Place on broiler pan and bake at 350 degrees for 1 hour. Turn at least one time while baking.

MEAT LOAF

1 pound ground beef
½ cup oatmeal (quick type)
1 small onion, finely chopped
1 clove garlic, pressed
4 tablespoons grated Parmesan cheese
2 teaspoons chopped parsley
1 can (8 ounces) tomato sauce
3 tablespoons Sebastiani Cabernet Sauvignon, or other dry, red wine
1 teaspoon salt
½ teaspoon pepper
½ teaspoon garlic salt
1 egg, beaten

Combine all ingredients, using only three-fourths of the tomato sauce. Shape into a greased loaf pan and pour remaining tomato sauce over loaf. Bake for 1 hour at 350 degrees.

Instead of the chopped onion, a half package of Lipton Onion Soup mix can be used. If you use the soup mix, reduce the amount of salt in this recipe to half a teaspoon.

Enjoy with a Sebastiani Pinot Noir or Merlot.

PORK LOIN ROAST

1 pork loin roast
2 cloves garlic, pressed
1 cup Sebastiani Chardonnay, or other dry, white wine
½ cup water
Salt, pepper to taste

Season roast with salt and pepper and rub with garlic. Place in roasting pan with wine and water. Bake at 325 degrees for 2 ½ hours, basting and turning occasionally. When roast is cooked, there should be enough liquid to add to the meat when it is served. If, while roasting, it looks as though there isn't enough liquid, add more wine.

Accompany this dish with a Sebastiani Barbera.

OSSO BUCO

I highly recommend Sebastiani
Barbera with this dish.

6 veal marrow bones with their meat, cut into pieces 3 inches long
4 tablespoons butter
4 tablespoons oil
1 small grated carrot
⅓ cup chopped celery
1 medium onion, chopped
1 clove garlic, chopped
Pinch of rosemary
Pinch of sage
4 tablespoons tomato sauce
1 cup Sebastiani Chardonnay, or other dry, white wine
½ cup water
Salt, pepper to taste

Brown veal in butter and oil, seasoning with salt and pepper. Brown on all sides, then turn pieces upright to hold in marrow. Add carrot, celery, onion, garlic, rosemary, and sage. Cover pot and simmer 10 minutes. Blend tomato sauce with wine and stir into veal. Add water and simmer over low heat, adding small amounts of water if necessary to prevent drying. Simmer until meat is tender, about 2 hours. Serve over boiled rice if desired.

Another method is to roll the veal slices after placing seasonings and prosciutto on them (eliminating the cheese) with the veal on the outside, and fasten the rolls with toothpicks. Sauté the rolls in butter and olive oil until they are thoroughly brown. Add white wine to the pan and simmer until veal is tender. Remove the toothpicks and serve the rolls on a heated platter with the sauce poured over them.

The rich flavors in this dish are complemented by a Sebastiani Chardonnay.

SALTIMBOCCA

Serves 4

8 thin veal cutlets
Salt, pepper, powdered sage to taste
4 thin slices prosciutto (Italian ham)
4 thin slices fontina cheese
4 tablespoons oil
6 tablespoons butter
8 fresh mushrooms, sliced or 2 cans (8 ounces each) mushrooms with liquid
4 teaspoons parsley, finely chopped
1 clove garlic, pressed
1 ½ cups Sebastiani Chardonnay or other dry, white wine

Season each cutlet with salt, pepper, and sage. On top of four cutlets, layer prosciutto and cheese and top with remaining cutlets. The veal should cover the prosciutto and cheese completely. Press edges of the veal together and seal by pounding with the flat of a cleaver. Secure with wooden picks. Brown both sides well in heated oil and 2 tablespoons butter, seasoning as you wish. Remove and place into a shallow, heated roasting pan. In a separate pan, sauté mushrooms, parsley, and garlic in butter. Add wine to the same pan used to cook the veal and simmer a few minutes. Add mushrooms and parsley and pour over meat. Add 4 tablespoons butter and cook until tender.

SIMA (STUFFED BREAST OF VEAL)

Serves 6–8

1 onion, chopped
4 tablespoons oil
2 tablespoons butter
2 cloves garlic, pressed
2 packages frozen chopped spinach or 2 bunches fresh spinach,
    well-cooked, drained, and finely chopped
½ cup chopped parsley
5 eggs
2 cups bread crumbs
¾ cup grated Parmesan cheese
Dash of basil
1 breast or shoulder of veal with a pocket cut in center
1 teaspoon rosemary
1 cup Sebastiani Chardonnay or other dry, white wine
⅓ cup butter
Salt, pepper to taste

Sauté onion in oil and butter, adding 1 clove garlic last. Add spinach, parsley, eggs, bread crumbs, cheese, and seasonings, mixing well with a fork. Stuff into pocket in veal and sew with a coarse needle and thread, closing completely. Place in roasting pan and rub with 1 clove garlic. Sprinkle with rosemary and baste with wine and butter. Roast uncovered at 350 degrees until brown, about 1 hour, basting occasionally.

VEAL SCALLOPINE

Serves 4

A Sebastiani Chardonnay or Pinot Noir is a perfect match for this dish.

1 ½ pounds veal scallops, cut 3/8 inch thick and pounded until ¼ inch thick
¼ teaspoon sage or 2 leaves fresh sage
Flour
2 tablespoons butter
4 tablespoons olive oil
¾ cup Sebastiani Chardonnay or other dry, white wine
1 small can button mushrooms with liquid (if you like mushrooms, use a larger can)
Juice of 1 lemon
4 tablespoons chopped parsley
Salt, pepper to taste

Season veal with sage, salt, and pepper. Dip in flour and shake off excess. In a heavy skillet, melt butter with oil. Add veal, 4 to 5 scallops at a time, and sauté them about 2 minutes on each side until they are golden brown. Transfer scallops to a plate. Pour off almost all fat from the skillet, leaving only a thin film on the bottom. Add wine, mushrooms, lemon juice, and parsley, and boil briskly 1–2 minutes, stirring constantly. Scrape in any browned bits clinging to the skillet. Return veal to skillet. Cover and simmer 10 to 15 minutes until veal is tender when pierced with the tip of a sharp knife.

BAKED CHUCK ROAST

Serves 6

This is a meal in itself—all that is needed to accompany this dish is a green salad. I have served this to guests, including the chef of one of Sonoma County's leading restaurants, adding sliced, cooked mushrooms on top...no one believed it was a chuck roast!

1 chuck roast (about 2 to 3 pounds)
1 clove garlic, pressed
1 package Lipton Onion Soup mix
2 potatoes
2 to 3 carrots
¼ cup Sebastiani Cabernet Sauvignon or other dry, red wine
Salt, pepper to taste

Line sides and bottom of a shallow roasting pan with heavy aluminum foil. Rub roast with garlic and season with salt and pepper. Place meat on foil and spread soup mix over roast. Peel and cut potatoes and carrots into good-sized chunks and place around roast. Salt and pepper vegetables. Take ends of foil and bring up over meat and vegetables. Pour wine over roast, then fold foil to keep it closed. Bake for 2 to 2 ½ hours at 350 degrees.

STUFFED FLANK STEAK

Serve with a Sebastiani Merlot.

1 ½ cups sliced fresh mushrooms or canned mushrooms
4 tablespoons butter
1 ½ cups Sebastiani Chardonnay or other dry, white wine
1 flank steak, pounded thin enough to roll
Bread Stuffing (see recipe on page 255; add 4 tablespoons pork sausage meat
    and 1 egg)
Flour
4 tablespoons oil
½ cup water
Salt, pepper, garlic powder to taste

Sauté mushrooms in 2 tablespoons butter with salt, pepper, and garlic powder to taste. Add ½ cup wine and simmer about 20 minutes. Season meat on all sides with salt, pepper, and garlic powder, then spread with stuffing. Roll lengthwise and tie securely with string about 2 inches apart. Dust roll generously with flour and brown well in oil and remaining butter. Add water and remaining wine, cover and simmer, turning occasionally, for about 1 hour or until tender when tested with a fork. Remove roll from pan and cool slightly so that when you slice it about 1 inch thick, the roll will stay together. Serve with a little gravy and sliced mushrooms.

SWISS STEAK

Serves 4–6

A Sebastiani Zinfandel pairs well with this classic dish.

2 pounds round steak
Flour
2 tablespoons oil
2 tablespoons butter
3 stalks celery, chopped
2 cloves garlic, pressed
1 small green bell pepper, cut into pieces
1 medium onion, chopped
1 teaspoon oregano
2 tablespoons chopped parsley
1 small can tomato sauce
1 cup Sebastiani Cabernet Sauvignon or other dry, red wine
1 can ripe olives
Salt, pepper to taste

Cut steak as desired, pound to tenderize, then dredge with flour that has been seasoned with salt and pepper. In a Dutch oven add meat, oil, seasoning to taste, and brown. Remove meat and add celery, garlic, bell pepper, onion, oregano, and parsley. Sauté lightly, then return meat and add tomato sauce. Cover with wine. Simmer 1 ½ hours over low heat until meat is tender, then add olives, and cook about 10 minutes longer. Serve over cooked rice.

TONGUE

This can be made up a day ahead as it is much better when re-heated.

1 beef tongue
2 bay leaves
1 onion
4 cloves
6 peppercorns
1 red chili pepper
1 tablespoon salt
Oil, vinegar, salt, pepper, chopped parsley, and garlic to taste

Wash tongue thoroughly and put in a large pot. Add bay leaves, onion, cloves, chili pepper, peppercorns, and salt. Add enough cold water just to cover meat and bring liquid to a slow boil, skimming frequently. Simmer covered over low heat for 3 hours until tongue is tender. Let tongue cool in water. Drain, peel off skin, and trim gristle and root away. Slice thin and serve cold with oil, vinegar, salt, pepper, chopped parsley, and garlic to taste.

TONGUE AND SPANISH SAUCE

A Sebastiani Chardonnay is a complementary tablemate.

4 tablespoons oil
2 tablespoons butter
1 small, dried onion, chopped
1 clove garlic, chopped
1 green bell pepper, chopped
3 stalks celery, chopped
1 small red chili pepper, chopped (optional)
1 can (16 ounces) tomatoes, chopped
½ cup Sebastiani Chardonnay or other dry, white wine
1 beef tongue (see recipe above for cooking instructions)
Salt, pepper to taste

In a deep pan, heat oil and butter. Add onions and brown, sprinkling with salt and bell pepper. Add garlic, bell peppers, celery, chili peppers, tomatoes, and wine. More salt and pepper may be added to suit your taste. Simmer 45 minutes to 1 hour. Then add sliced tongue and heat thoroughly.

TRIPE

Serves 6–8

A Sebastiani Pinot Noir or Chardonnay is recommended to enhance the flavors of the meat.

1 ½ to 2 pounds tripe
4 tablespoons oil
2 tablespoons butter
1 onion, chopped
1 clove garlic, chopped
2 teaspoon chopped parsley
¼ cup dried Italian mushrooms (optional)
1 can (8 ounces) tomato sauce
1 cup Sebastiani Chardonnay or other dry, white wine
Dash of cayenne pepper
1 medium potato, cut into ½ inch cubes
Grated Parmesan cheese
Salt, pepper to taste

Cut tripe into strips 3 inches long and ½ inch wide. In a saucepan, heat oil and butter and sauté onion, taking care not to let it brown. Add salt and pepper to taste. Add garlic, parsley, mushrooms, and tomato sauce. Place tripe into saucepan and add wine. Add enough water to cover tripe completely. Stir all ingredients and cover, after adding cayenne pepper. Simmer for 1 ½ hours; then add potato and continue cooking until potato and tripe are tender. Sprinkle with cheese when serving.

BREADED VEAL CUTLETS

6 veal steaks or chops
2 eggs, beaten with a fork
Cracker crumbs mixed with 3 tablespoons grated Parmesan cheese
4 tablespoons olive oil
2 tablespoons butter
Lemon wedges
Salt, pepper, garlic salt to taste

Season steaks or chops generously with salt, pepper, and garlic salt. Dip into eggs, then dip into seasoned cracker crumbs. Place in shallow baking dish along with oil and butter. Brown at 360 degrees until tender, turning once so that both sides are browned. Takes about 15 to 20 minutes on each side. Serve with lemon wedges.

VEAL SAUTÉED WITH OLIVES

1 ½ pounds veal, cut like stew meat
4 tablespoons olive oil
2 tablespoons butter
Salt, pepper, garlic salt to taste
1 clove garlic, pressed
2 tablespoons chopped parsley
¼ teaspoon sage
¾ cup Sebastiani Chardonnay, or other dry, white wine
½ cup hard green olives

Brown veal in oil and butter, adding salt, pepper, and garlic salt to all sides. Turn frequently with spatula until brown. Add garlic, parsley, sage, and heated wine. Add olives and cover. Simmer for 20 minutes or until veal is tender. Add more wine if you wish the veal to be more moist.

Cappretto (kid goat) is good cooked this way, too. Sometimes I use the dark, dry olives in place of the green.

VEAL PARMIGIANO

Serves 4–6

4 to 6 veal steaks, round
2 eggs, beaten
⅔ cup cracker meal
4 tablespoons oil
2 tablespoons butter
4 tablespoons grated Parmesan cheese
Spaghetti Sauce (see recipe on page 72)
4 tablespoons Sebastiani Chardonnay or other dry, white wine
4 to 6 slices Monterey Jack cheese
Salt, pepper to taste

Dip veal steaks into eggs, adding salt and pepper. After this, dip into cracker meal on both sides. Brown veal on both sides in oil and butter, adding salt and pepper to both sides. Place in shallow baking pan, sprinkle with Parmesan, and cover with spaghetti sauce and wine. Bake at 325 degrees for 30 minutes or until veal is tender. Just before serving, add a slice of Monterey Jack cheese over each steak. More sauce may be added, if desired.

VEAL PAPRIKA IN NOODLE RING

Serves 8

4 pounds veal shoulder, cut into 1 ½ inch cubes
¼ cup butter
¼ cup oil
2 teaspoons salt
1 tablespoon sugar
4 teaspoons curry powder
1 ¼ teaspoons pepper
¼ teaspoon paprika
1 can (10 or 12 ounces) condensed beef broth, undiluted
2 ½ cups sour cream
⅔ cup flour
⅔ cup cold water
1 cup snipped parsley
1 package (8 ounces) broad noodles
¼ cup slivered almonds, toasted
1 ½ teaspoons poppy seeds

About 2 hours before dinner, brown one-third of the veal cubes in hot butter and oil. Remove to plate and repeat twice more. Combine in Dutch oven and sprinkle with salt, sugar, curry, pepper, and paprika. Add broth, sour cream, and stir in flour blended smooth with water; add parsley. Simmer with cover on for 1 hour, stirring occasionally until veal is tender. Cook noodles as directed on package and let drain well. About 30 minutes before dinner, heat oven to 350 degrees. Arrange cooked noodles around edges of a shallow baking dish. Spoon veal mixture into center and top with almonds and poppy seeds. Cover with foil and bake 15 minutes.

Chicken Almond, page 140

POULTRY

CHICKEN ALMOND

Serves 8

4 pounds chicken breasts or 2 broilers, cut up
Flour seasoned with salt and pepper
4 tablespoons oil
2 tablespoons butter
2 onions, chopped
2 green bell peppers, chopped
1 clove garlic, chopped
3 ½ teaspoons curry powder
½ teaspoon white pepper
½ teaspoon thyme
1 can (28 ounces) solid pack tomatoes, mashed
1 tablespoon chopped parsley
¼ cup toasted almonds
¾ cup Sebastiani Chardonnay, or other dry, white wine
6 cups cooked rice
Salt, pepper to taste

Roll chicken in seasoned flour and brown in oil and butter. Remove chicken pieces. Add onions, bell peppers, and garlic, stirring well and adding remaining seasoning and salt and pepper to taste. Then add tomatoes and parsley and heat thoroughly. Place in a greased casserole dish and add almonds and wine, mixing well. Cover and bake at 350 degrees for 45 minutes. Serve over rice.

CHICKEN BORDEAUX

Serves 4–6

2 tablespoons butter
2 tablespoons olive oil
1 fryer, cut up
1 tablespoon chopped parsley
2 cloves garlic, pressed
1 tablespoon minced onion
1 cup Sebastiani Chardonnay, or other dry, white wine
1 package frozen artichoke hearts
1 can (6 ounces) whole mushrooms with liquid
Salt, pepper to taste

Heat butter and oil together and cook chicken pieces until golden brown, seasoning well with salt and pepper. Sprinkle with parsley, then cover, and cook slowly 8 to 9 minutes. Remove chicken pieces and keep warm. Add garlic, onion, wine, artichokes, and mushrooms to the juices in the pan. Bring to a boil and cook 1 minute longer. Return chicken to pan, reheat, and serve immediately.

CHICKEN IN SHERRY SAUCE

Serves 6

6 chicken breasts
Salt, pepper to taste
½ cup dry sherry or cream sherry (or Sebastiani Symphony)
1 can cream of mushroom soup
½ pint sour cream

Sprinkle chicken with salt and pepper and lay in baking pan. Mix sherry, soup, and sour cream together well and pour over chicken. Bake for 1 hour and 10 minutes in 350 degree oven.

Chicken Cacciatore a la Lombarda, opposite page

CHICKEN CACCIATORE A LA LOMBARDA

Serves 4–6

Pheasant can also be prepared according to this recipe. Cooking time will depend upon the size and age of the pheasant; it may take anywhere from 1 to 2 hours. This cacciatore dish goes well with polenta. Serve over polenta and top all with grated Parmesan cheese.

We recommend a Sebastiani Chardonnay with this dish.

1 chicken, cut into pieces
2 tablespoons flour
4 tablespoons olive oil
2 tablespoons butter
½ onion, chopped
1 stalk celery, chopped
1 clove garlic, pressed
1 tablespoon chopped parsley
1 small can sliced button mushrooms
1 ½ cups Sebastiani Chardonnay, or other dry, white wine
½ teaspoon thyme
½ teaspoon rosemary
Salt, pepper to taste

Dust chicken lightly with flour. Brown well in oil and butter, sprinkling all sides with salt and pepper, while cooking. Add onion and celery and salt and pepper to taste. Stir frequently with pancake turner until celery and onion are limp. Then add garlic and parsley, stirring constantly. Add mushrooms, wine, thyme, and rosemary. Cover and simmer for about 45 minutes. If there is too much liquid, cook without cover for the last 10 to 15 minutes.

CHICKEN WITH WINE AND MUSHROOMS

Serves 4–6

I use a Sebastiani Chardonnay both in cooking and for drinking with this meal.

1 fryer, cut up
Salt, pepper, garlic salt, paprika to taste
4 tablespoons butter
6 tablespoons olive oil
1 can sliced button mushrooms with liquid
¾ cup Sebastiani Chardonnay, or other dry, white wine
1 or 2 cloves garlic, chopped (optional)
2 or 3 sprigs rosemary (optional)

Season chicken pieces generously with salt, pepper, garlic salt, and paprika. Melt butter and oil in shallow roasting pan and place chicken pieces in pan. Place pan in 350 degree oven and turn pieces as they brown. Heat mushrooms with liquid in wine. After 30 minutes, add to chicken. If desired, garlic and rosemary may be added, but remove before serving. Continue cooking until tender, about 15 to 20 minutes.

ROAST CHICKEN

We recommend the Sebastiani Chardonnay with this dish.

1 roasting chicken, any size
Salt, pepper, garlic salt to taste
1 sprig thyme
1 sprig rosemary
1 clove garlic, mashed
½ dry onion, cut into 4 pieces
Oil
Butter
1 to 1 ½ cups Sebastiani Chardonnay, or other dry, white wine

Sprinkle chicken generously with salt, pepper, and garlic salt. Be sure to cover all sides and inside the cavity. Place thyme, rosemary, garlic, and onion inside chicken. Place in shallow roasting pan with a little oil and butter. Cook at 350 degrees and baste occasionally until slightly brown, about 30 minutes. Then add wine that has been heated, not boiled, and baste occasionally until done. A 4 pound chicken will take about 1 hour and 15 minutes.

MANGIAMO The Sebastiani Family Cookbook

CHILIED CHICKEN

Serves 4

1 package tortillas
⅔ cup milk
1 can diced Ortega chilies
1 small onion, chopped
1 can cream of chicken soup
1 can cream of mushroom soup
1 can chopped olives
¾ pound Tillamook cheese
4 large chicken breasts, cooked, boned, and cut up

Soak tortillas in milk. Make sauce by mixing chilies, onion, soups, olives, and cheese. Add chicken pieces. Drain tortillas. Layer tortillas and chicken mixture in a greased casserole dish. If desired, the milk from the tortillas may be mixed with the chili sauce. Bake at 350 degrees for 30 minutes.

This Chilied Chicken goes well with a Sebastiani Pinot Noir.

NONA'S CHICKEN

Serves 10–12

2 chickens, cut into large pieces
Garlic salt
Flour
2 tablespoons olive oil
6 tablespoons butter
½ cup chopped parsley
1 can sliced mushrooms, drained (optional)
⅛ teaspoon minced red chili peppers
Rosemary
Thyme
1 cup Sebastiani Chardonnay, or other dry, white wine
Salt, pepper to taste

A Sebastiani Chardonnay (chilled) goes especially well with this chicken dish.

Season chicken with salt, pepper, and garlic salt. Dust lightly with flour, then place pieces in shallow baking pan or on cookie sheet, sprinkling over oil and

Recipe continued on following page

melted butter. Brown chicken under broiler, turning all sides to brown. After browning, layer pieces in a deep, greased casserole, sprinkling each layer with parsley, mushrooms, chili peppers, rosemary, thyme, and salt and pepper to taste. Pour over remaining pan juices and wine. Cover and bake at 325 degrees for 1 to 1 ½ hours until chicken is tender.

CHICKEN GIBLET SAUTÉ

Serves 4

1 ½ pounds chicken giblets
1 tablespoon flour
½ teaspoon salt
1 tablespoons butter
2 tablespoons olive oil
1 clove garlic, pressed
½ cup water
1 cup Sebastiani Chardonnay, or other dry, white wine
1 small can mushrooms (optional)
Grated Parmesan cheese (optional)
Salt, pepper to taste

Roll giblets in flour seasoned with salt and pepper. Melt butter with oil and garlic in a saucepan and add giblets, stirring well. Sauté giblets until brown, then add water, wine, and mushrooms. Cover and stir occasionally until tender, about 25 to 30 minutes. More salt and wine may be added if needed. Sprinkle with cheese before serving over boiled rice or noodles.

When I start to roast a turkey, I like to cover it with a large, heavy paper shopping bag. Simply cut out one side of the bag and place over turkey. This produces a very golden finish on the bird.

This classic is wonderful anytime of the year with a Sebastiani Symphony or Sebastiani Eye of the Swan (Pinot Noir Blanc) and shared among friends and family.

TURKEY AND TURKEY DRESSING

1 roasting turkey
Dry bread cubes from 1 loaf of sour French bread
½ cup chopped parsley
½ cup grated Parmesan cheese
1 or 2 teaspoons poultry seasoning
2 teaspoons salt
1 teaspoon pepper
1 teaspoon garlic salt
½ cup butter
2 onions, chopped
½ bunch celery, chopped
2 cloves garlic, chopped
1 to 2 cups broth (see below)
Salt, pepper, garlic salt to taste

Broth:
Turkey neck
Turkey giblets
Salted water
¼ onion
1 stalk celery
1 clove garlic
1 ½ cups Sebastiani Chardonnay, or other dry, white wine
1 ½ cups melted butter

In a large bowl, combine bread cubes, parsley, cheese, and seasonings. In a large saucepan, melt butter, sauté onions, and celery, sprinkling with salt, pepper, and garlic salt to taste. Add garlic and sauté lightly. In a stockpot, prepare broth by boiling neck and giblets in salted water with onion, celery, and garlic. Let cool. Add cooled broth to sautéed onion-celery mixture, then mix well into bread-cube mixture.

Rub turkey with olive oil and season generously with salt, pepper, and garlic salt. Stuff with dressing. When turkey is ready for baking, place in a shallow oiled roasting pan and baste occasionally while cooking with wine and butter. Cook at 325 degrees. Turkey is cooked when leg joints move freely. Remove from oven and let sit at least 1 hour before carving. Cover with foil to keep warm. This procedure makes it much easier to carve the turkey and keeps the meat moist.

GAME

Wild Duck Antoinette, page 158

CORNISH GAME HEN IN CASSEROLE

A Sebastiani Zinfandel pairs well with this dish.

6 game hens, split
¼ cup flour
4 tablespoons butter
4 tablespoons olive oil
I cup chicken broth
I can cream of chicken soup
½ cup Sebastiani Chardonnay, or other dry, white wine
I cup sour cream
Pepper to taste

Dust game hens with flour and sauté in butter and oil for 10 minutes or until brown. Remove from skillet and arrange in casserole dish. Add chicken broth to butter and oil in skillet, stir well, and pour over game hens. Cover casserole and bake at 325 degrees for 30 minutes. Take game hens out of casserole and stir chicken soup, wine, and sour cream into sauce in casserole. Add pepper to taste and return game hens to casserole dish. Bake in 350 degree oven uncovered for 15 to 20 minutes, or until heated thoroughly.

DOVES

Sometimes I vary this recipe by adding ½ chopped onion and ½ cup tomato sauce. This makes a great dish when served over polenta.

6 to 8 doves
I to 2 tablespoons flour
4 tablespoons olive oil
2 tablespoons butter
2 cloves garlic, chopped
2 teaspoons chopped parsley
I ½ cups Sebastiani Chardonnay, or other dry, white wine
Thyme, rosemary, salt, pepper to taste

Sprinkle doves with salt and pepper on all sides and in cavities. Dust lightly with flour and brown well in oil and butter. Add garlic, parsley, thyme, and rosemary, and brown slightly. Add warmed wine and simmer, covered, until doves are tender, about 30 minutes, or more, if necessary.

GAME SAUCE

1 cube butter
4 tablespoons ketchup
Juice of 1 lemon
2 tablespoons Worcestershire
2 tablespoons Heinz 57 Steak Sauce
4 tablespoons Sebastiani Cabernet Sauvignon or Zinfandel, or other dry,
    red wine

Melt butter in saucepan. Add remaining ingredients. Cook 10 minutes and serve. This sauce is excellent over wild duck or wild goose.

VENISON OR BEEF JERKY

Slices of venison or beef, ½ inch thick and 4 inches long
Salt, pepper to taste

Season meat slices with salt and pepper. Put into a pan and refrigerate over night. Pour off any liquid before stringing with heavy thread. Hang lines of meat in a wire mesh cage and place cage in direct sunlight for 4 to 5 days. At evening, place a canvas over the cage so that the meat does not absorb any moisture. Store in a tin covered with cheesecloth or paper. Keeps for several months.

For *Oven-Cured Jerky*: Use same ingredients and follow instructions, except instead of outdoor curing, place meat on oven racks and put into oven at lowest possible temperature. Turn oven on for 1 hour and off for 1 hour, for about 12 hours, or until meat is dried.

STEWED RABBIT

Serves 4

Polenta serves as a good accompaniment to this dish.

Serve with a Sebastiani Merlot.

2 tablespoons olive oil
2 tablespoons butter
1 rabbit (3 pounds), cut into pieces
1 onion, chopped
1 small green bell pepper, chopped
2 stalks celery, chopped
1 clove garlic
1 can (8 ounces) tomato sauce
1 can (8 ounces) tomatoes, peeled and chopped
1 sprig rosemary or 1/4 teaspoon dry rosemary
1 cup Sebastiani Chardonnay, or other dry, white wine
Salt, pepper to taste

In a Dutch oven or deep frying pan, heat butter and oil. Brown rabbit, adding salt and pepper on all sides. Remove rabbit and set aside. Brown onion, bell pepper, and celery with a little more salt and pepper, adding garlic lastly. Add tomato sauce, tomatoes, rosemary, and wine. Cook slowly for 30 minutes, uncovered. Return rabbit to sauce. Cover and cook about 45 minutes until rabbit is tender.

SQUABS IN WHITE WINE

Serves 6–8

6 squabs or small chickens
3 tablespoons olive oil
3 tablespoons butter
1 ½ cups Sebastiani Chardonnay, or other dry, white wine
6 squab livers
2 chicken livers
8 shallots, finely chopped
1 can (8 ounces) sliced button mushrooms with liquid
Chopped parsley
Salt, pepper to taste

In a shallow roasting pan with olive oil and butter, place birds that have been seasoned with salt and pepper on all sides. Brown in 350 degree oven for 30 minutes. Pour heated wine over birds and cook 15 minutes longer. Add birds' livers, shallots, and mushrooms with their liquid. Cook for an additional 15 minutes until birds are tender. Transfer birds to a heated plate, pour pan juices over them, and sprinkle with parsley.

VENISON HEART

Serves 4

1 deer heart, cut into ¼ inch slices
Flour
3 tablespoons butter
3 tablespoons olive oil
Salt, pepper to taste

Season heart slices with salt and pepper, then dip into flour. Heat butter and oil in frying pan and fry 3 to 4 minutes on each side. Pour over pan juices before serving.

We like to serve this dish with a Sebastiani Zinfandel.

Cornish Game Hen in Casserole, page 150

VENISON LIVER

Serves 4

1 pound venison liver, thinly sliced (you can substitute calf's liver)
Flour
3 tablespoons butter
3 tablespoons olive oil
2 teaspoons chopped parsley
Salt, pepper to taste

Season liver slices with salt and pepper and dip into flour. Heat butter and oil in frying pan and sauté liver slices quickly, 1 to 2 minutes on each side. Do not overcook liver as it gets tough. Pour over pan juices and sprinkle with chopped parsley before serving.

VENISON SCALLOPINE

Serves 4

I like to accompany this dish with Sebastiani Cabernet Sauvignon.

1 ½ pound piece venison steak
Flour seasoned with salt and pepper
4 tablespoons olive oil
2 tablespoons butter
1 clove garlic, minced
Sage
Thyme
½ cup Sebastiani Chardonnay, or other dry, white wine
½ cup water
Salt, pepper to taste

Slice venison into serving-size pieces and pound well. Coat pieces well with flour mixture. Heat oil and butter in frying pan, then add venison and brown on both sides. Add garlic and season to taste with salt and pepper. Sprinkle with sage and thyme. Pour over wine and water, then cover, and bake at 350 degrees for 45 minutes to 1 hour until tender.

VENISON POT ROAST

¼ cup wine vinegar
1 venison pot roast (about 4 to 6 pounds)
1 teaspoon salt
1 teaspoon pepper
1 teaspoon onion salt
1 teaspoon garlic salt
1 teaspoon celery salt
2 onions, chopped
2 to 3 cloves garlic, chopped
½ teaspoon thyme
½ teaspoon chopped basil
½ teaspoon paprika
1 pinch chopped red chili
1 can solid pack tomatoes, chopped
2 cups Sebastiani Cabernet Sauvignon, or other dry, red wine
2 teaspoons Worcestershire sauce

Saturate a cloth with vinegar; wring out and wipe meat thoroughly. Heat oil in heavy skillet or Dutch oven. Brown meat slowly on all sides; add salt, pepper, onion salt, garlic salt, and celery salt while browning meat. Then add onion and brown, stirring frequently. Add remaining ingredients, making sure wine is heated, cover, and cook for 2 ½ to 3 hours.

VENISON STEW

Serves 6

This stew is delightful served over rice or noodles and with a green salad—it makes a very nourishing dinner, and it is also very good made with either beef, veal, lamb, or goat.

Serve with the Sebastiani Merlot or Zinfandel left over from cooking.

1 ½ pounds venison, cut into 1 ½ inch cubes
2 tablespoons flour
½ teaspoon salt
½ teaspoon pepper
½ teaspoon garlic salt
¼ cup oil
¼ cup butter
2 stalks celery, chopped
1 onion, chopped
2 cloves garlic, pressed
4 sprigs parsley, chopped
½ teaspoon thyme
½ teaspoon sage
1 ½ cups Sebastiani Merlot or Zinfandel, other dry, red wine
½ cup water

Coat venison in flour seasoned with salt, pepper, and garlic salt. Brown well in oil and butter, adding celery and onion. Add garlic and parsley and brown slightly. Add thyme and sage; then pour wine and water over all. Simmer, covered, over low heat or in a 325 degree oven for 1 to 1½ hours until meat is tender.

I have probably cooked more ducks than any one I know, but few cooks agree on how to serve roast wild duck. There is no doubt that a duck on the rare side is more tender and juicy than one that has been cooked well-done. However, there is no need to apologize if you don't like rare duck—just cook them a little longer. I do hope you have a self-cleaning oven.

Goes well with a Sebastiani Pinot Noir.

The perfect accompaniment with duck prepared in this manner is a good green salad with olive oil and vinegar.

Serve with a bottle of Sebastiani Pinot Noir or Sebastiani's Eye of the Swan.

ROAST WILD DUCK

1 duck
Juice of 1 lemon
1 green onion, whole
1 stalk of tender celery with leaves
1 clove garlic, mashed
1 sprig parsley (optional)
¼ apple
1 sprig thyme
2 tablespoons Heinz 57 Steak Sauce (optional)
Salt, pepper to taste

Rub duck with lemon juice on all sides. Salt and pepper generously on all sides and in cavity. Place remaining ingredients inside bird's cavity. Place on broiler pan and put into 500 degree oven. If cooking more than one duck at a time, do not put them too close together. Cook large ducks (mallards) 20 to 25 minutes; medium ducks (sprig) 15 to 18 minutes; small ducks (teals) 12 to 15 minutes. Ducks will be just slightly on the pink side, but not rare.

WILD DUCK ANTOINETTE

Serves 2

1 duck
Garlic salt
Thyme, fresh or powdered
Flour
1 pint vegetable oil
Salt, pepper to taste

If your duck is large, like a mallard, canvasback, or sprig, cut into 6 parts. If your duck is smaller, cut into 4 pieces. Generously sprinkle garlic salt, thyme, salt and pepper over duck pieces, then dip into flour. Deep-fry ducks in a 10-inch frying pan in vegetable oil. Fry 10 to 15 minutes, depending on how you like your duck. If you use fresh thyme, add 2 or 3 sprigs after duck has been frying about 5 minutes and turn once.

ROAST WILD GOOSE

Serves 3–4 (depending on the size of the goose)

Sebastiani Barbera goes well with this dish.

1 wild goose, cleaned and dressed
Juice of 1 lemon
Salt, pepper, garlic salt to taste
2 green onions, whole
1 stalk celery (tender part with green)
1 clove garlic, mashed
1 sprig rosemary or thyme
4 tablespoons oil
½ cup Sebastiani Barbera, or other dry, red wine
½ cup Sebastiani Chardonnay, or other dry, white wine

Rub goose with lemon juice; then sprinkle salt, pepper, and garlic salt on all sides and in cavity. Place onions, celery, garlic, and rosemary in cavity. Place in a deep Dutch oven along with oil. Roast, uncovered, for 20 minutes at 400 degrees. Add heated wine and cover, reducing heat to 350 degrees. Cook until goose is tender when tested with a fork. May take anywhere from 2 to 2 ½ hours, depending on the age of the goose. Baste goose 2 or 3 times while baking. You may need to add more wine if there isn't enough juice.

SALADS

Caesar Salad, page 166

salad tips

1. When washing lettuce, squeeze the juice of 1 or 2 lemons into the water and also add about 1/2 teaspoon salt. The lemon juice adds to the crispness of the lettuce and the salt will drive out any insects hidden in the lettuce leaves.

2. If lettuce seems to be limp, add ice cubes to the water and allow lettuce to soak a few minutes.

3. After thorough washing, dry lettuce leaves thoroughly between towels or drain well in a salad basket.

4. Always chill lettuce after it is cleaned. Put in a cloth bag or other closed container in refrigerator to keep cold and crispy.

5. If you wish tomatoes to be added to a salad, prepare them separately and use them as garnish. If they are added along with the other ingredients, their juice will thin the dressing.

6. It is best to cut tomatoes in vertical slices because they bleed less this way.

7. A tastier tossed salad will result if several kinds of lettuce are used.

8. Always taste a tossed salad before serving. If it seems dull, add a little more vinegar or salt and pepper.

9. For molded salads, always rinse mold out with cold water before using. To unmold, dip mold in hot water, shake until loose, and unmold quickly.

10. Chill salad plates (bowls), especially if serving individual salads.

11. For a change of pace, try chilling the salad forks, too. You'll be amazed at the reations you'll receive.

APRICOT-PISTACHE SALAD

Serves 6

2 to 3 ounce packages cream cheese
1 tablespoon cream
½ cup finely chopped pistachio nuts
Pinch of salt (optional)
18 canned apricot halves
1 small head lettuce
½ cup French dressing
1 tablespoon bottled lime juice

Mash cream cheese with cream until smooth. Add nuts and salt. Form this mixture into 18 balls, ¾ inch in diameter. Arrange 3 apricot halves, round side down, on each of 6 individual beds of lettuce. Place a cheese ball in the center of each half and serve with French dressing mixed with lime juice.

BEAN AND TUNA SALAD

Serves 4–6

1 can red kidney beans
1/2 red dry onion, chopped
1 can (6 1/2 ounces) tuna
4 tablespoons oil
2 tablespoons finely chopped parsley
1 clove garlic, minced
Wine vinegar
Salt, pepper to taste

Drain and wash kidney beans in a colander. Mix all ingredients in a bowl, adding salt and pepper to taste. Chill and serve.

This salad is great for barbeques during the summer months. Serve with a Sebastiani Chardonnay.

BENGAL SALAD

Serves 6

This salad is marvelous for lunching on a hot day. It can be made up the day before serving, if the crab and shrimp are withheld.

1 cup crab legs
1 cup shrimp
1 ½ cups finely chopped onion
1 cup diced celery
½ cup sliced water chestnuts
1 can (13 ½ ounce) pineapple tidbits, drained
1 ½ cups chopped pimiento
2 tablespoons currants
juice of 1 lemon
4 tablespoons chutney
Salt to taste

Dressing:
1 cup mayonnaise
½ cup sour cream
½ teaspoon curry powder

Combine all ingredients in the order given and mix together well. Mix dressing ingredients and pour over the crab-shrimp mixture. Toss well.

FRUIT COCKTAIL WITH WINE

Serves 6–8

Excellent as a first course for a Thanksgiving or Christmas meal while waiting for the other courses.

2 cans fruit cocktail, any size
1 can Mandarin oranges
Fresh fruit on hand, e.g. apples, bananas, peaches
1 sprig mint
¼ cup Sebastiani Symphony or other sweet, white wine

Mix all ingredients together and chill well. Serve as a fruit cup for a first course instead of a salad.

ORANGE GELATIN SALAD

Serves 12

2 packages orange gelatin
1 cup boiling water
2 cans mandarin oranges, save juice
1 pint orange sherbet
1 cup sour cream
1 can (13 ounces) pineapple tidbits

Dissolve gelatin in boiling water. Add juice from oranges and chill until mixture begins to gel. Add sherbet and sour cream and beat until frothy. Add pineapple and orange. Pour into mold and chill overnight.

CELERY VICTOR

Serves 4

1 cup well-seasoned French dressing
1 can hearts of celery, well-drained
1 small head lettuce, shredded
Coarsely ground black pepper
8 anchovy filets
2 grated hard-boiled eggs
1 avocado, sliced (optional)
1 tomato, sliced (optional)

Pour French dressing over celery hearts and let chill several hours. Drain off most of dressing and place celery on shredded lettuce. Sprinkle with pepper, place anchovies on top, and cover with grated egg. Avocado and tomato may be used for extra garnish, if so desired.

CAESAR SALAD

Serves 12

1 clove garlic
½ to ¾ cup olive oil or other salad oil
2 cups garlic croutons
2 large heads romaine lettuce
¾ teaspoon salt
Generous gratings of black pepper
1 ½ teaspoons Worcestershire sauce
¼ teaspoon dry mustard
2 eggs, boiled 1 1⁄2 minutes
Juice of 1 lemon
6 to 8 anchovy filets, finely chopped
½ cup grated Parmesan cheese

Crush garlic and pour into ½ cup oil; add croutons and set aside. Tear lettuce into large salad bowl, sprinkle salt, and add pepper. Mix Worcestershire and mustard with remaining oil and pour over lettuce; tossing well. Break eggs into salad. Add lemon juice and toss thoroughly. Add anchovies and cheese and toss again. Add croutons, lastly, toss gently, and serve immediately.

CRAB SALAD

Serves 6

1 can (10 ¾ ounces) tomato soup
2 small packages cream cheese
3 tablespoons unflavored gelatin softened in ½ cup cold water
¾ teaspoon salt
½ green bell pepper, finely chopped
1 cup finely chopped celery
1 small onion, finely chopped
1 large can crabmeat
1 cup mayonnaise

Heat soup; add cream cheese and gelatin. Blend well. Add salt, bell pepper, celery, onion, crab, and mayonnaise to mixture. Pour into mold, chill, and serve cold.

Enjoy with a Sebastiani Symphony.

Try this salad with a glass of Sebastiani Chardonnay.

CRANBERRY SALAD

Serves 8–10

2 packages cherry gelatin
2 cups boiling water
1 ½ cups sugar
Juice of 1 orange
Juice of 1 lemon
1 package raw cranberries, chopped
1 cup chopped nuts
1 red apple, unpeeled and chopped
2 cups chopped celery

Dissolve gelatin in boiling water. Add sugar, orange juice, and lemon juice. Then add cranberries, nuts, apple, and celery, mixing well. Chill in large mold or individual molds.

BASIC FRENCH DRESSING

Makes about 2 cups

¾ teaspoon salt
½ teaspoon black pepper
½ teaspoon dry mustard
1 clove garlic
½ cup wine vinegar
1 ½ cups olive oil

Add salt, pepper, mustard, and garlic to vinegar. Stir well with a fork, then add oil. Beat well until dressing thickens. Remove garlic before using.

This dressing can be easily made up ahead of time and refrigerated, but be sure to remove the clove of garlic after 24 hours. Also, if dressing is refrigerated, let stand at room temperature for 30 minutes before serving so the ingredients have a chance to blend.

GREEN GODDESS SALAD

Serves 6

5 anchovy filets (anchovy paste may be used instead)
2 green onions, chopped
¼ cup minced parsley
1 clove garlic
1 large head lettuce
1 ½ cups mayonnaise
2 tablespoons tarragon vinegar
1 pound cooked lobster, shrimp, or crab meat (optional)

Chop anchovies and onions together until finely minced; then add parsley. Rub a salad bowl with garlic and cut lettuce into bite-sized pieces, then place into bowl. Stir mayonnaise and vinegar into the anchovy mixture and mix well. Pour over lettuce, tossing thoroughly. Spoon onto individual salad plates and garnish with shellfish, if desired.

GELATIN RIBBON SALAD

Serves 8

2 packages cherry gelatin
4 to 5 cups boiling water
#2 ½ size can fruit salad, reserve juice
1 package lemon gelatin
1 cup mayonnaise
2 small packages cream cheese

Dissolve 1 package cherry gelatin in 2 cups water. Put in bottom of pan with drained fruit salad and set until firm. Dissolve lemon gelatin in reserved juice from fruit and add enough boiling water to make 2 cups. Blend mayonnaise and cream cheese; add to lemon gelatin when it begins to congeal. Spread on top of firm cherry gelatin. Dissolve other package of cherry gelatin in 2 cups boiling water and place on top of lemon gelatin mixture. Chill until firm.

MIXED GREEN SALAD

Serves 8–10

1 head romaine lettuce, heart only
1 head endive
1 head butter lettuce
2 to 10 radishes, thinly sliced
3 stalks celery heart, chopped
2 green onions, chopped
Grated Parmesan cheese (optional)

Dressing:
2 anchovy filets
1 tablespoon wine vinegar
3 tablespoons olive oil
¼ teaspoon dry mustard
1 clove garlic, mashed
Salt, pepper to taste

Wash and clean all lettuce and let drain thoroughly. Break into bite-sized pieces and mix with radishes, celery, and onion in salad bowl. Chop anchovies and combine with remaining ingredients. Beat with a fork until dressing thickens. Pour over salad and toss lightly. Sprinkle with Parmesan cheese, if desired.

There are many ways to vary a mixed green salad. Here are just a few suggestions: 1) add onion rings; 2) add sliced raw mushrooms; 3) add cubes of avocado; 4) add peeled, sliced cucumbers; 5) add cooked crab or shrimp; 6) add strips of cold chicken, turkey, ham, or shredded tuna.

Marinated Beans Salad, opposite page

MARINATED BEANS SALAD

Serves 12–15

Serve with a glass of Sebastiani Pinot Noir.

#303 size can green beans, undrained
1 can wax beans, undrained
1 can kidney beans, drained and rinsed
1 can garbanzo beans, drained
1 can okra, drained
½ cup sugar
⅔ cup apple cider vinegar
⅔ cup oil
1 teaspoon salt
½ teaspoon pepper
½ cup finely chopped green bell peppers
2 medium onions, cut into thin rings

Mix all beans with sugar, vinegar, oil, salt, and pepper. Then add green peppers and onions. Chill.

MARY ANN'S SHRIMP SALAD

Serves 4

1 head romaine lettuce
1 can (4 ½ ounces) shrimp, well-drained
1 cup mayonnaise
1 tablespoon white vinegar
1 teaspoon dry mustard
½ teaspoon beau monde seasoning
½ teaspoon lemon celery seasoning
3 tablespoons ketchup
2 hard-boiled eggs, chopped
1 sweet pickle, finely chopped (optional)
Salt, white pepper, garlic salt to taste

Trim both ends from head of lettuce. Leaving head intact, cut into quarters lengthwise and place each quarter on an individual plate. Combine remaining ingredients and pour over each quarter of lettuce.

ORANGE-LEMON PUDDING SALAD

Serves 8–10

2 ½ cups boiling water
2 packages orange gelatin
1 can (6 ounces) frozen orange juice, thawed
1 can mandarin oranges, drained
1 cup crushed pineapple, drained
1 package lemon pie filling
½ pint whipping cream

Add boiling water to gelatin. Then add orange juice, oranges, and pineapple. Set until firm. Mix pie filling and cook as directed on package. Let cool. Whip cream and fold into the cooled lemon filling. Spread this over the orange gelatin mixture.

PINEAPPLE-COTTAGE CHEESE SALAD

Serves 8–10

Perfect served with a
Sebastiani Symphony.

1 package lime gelatin
1 package lemon gelatin
2 cups boiling water
1 cup canned milk
1 pint cottage cheese, small curd
1 can crushed pineapple
1 cup chopped nuts (walnuts or almonds)
1 tablespoon horseradish (optional)
1 cup mayonnaise

Mix lime gelatin and lemon gelatin together; add water and stir until gelatin is dissolved. Add milk, cottage cheese, pineapple, nuts, and horseradish to gelatin mixture and blend well. Finally, add mayonnaise and pour entire mixture into a mold. (A 13 x 8 rectangular baking dish works well.) Chill and serve.

POTATO SALAD

Serves 10

4 or 5 medium potatoes
4 or 5 tablespoons white vinegar
3 hard-boiled eggs, chopped
½ onion, chopped
4 stalks celery, very finely chopped
½ cup parsley, chopped
1 small pimento, chopped
Salt, pepper, garlic salt to taste
1 cup mayonnaise
1 teaspoon dry mustard
Paprika
8 olives
Few sprigs parsley

Boil potatoes with skins on in uncovered pot until tender, making sure all potatoes are covered with water. Drain, peel, and slice potatoes, then marinate them well with vinegar. Add eggs, onion, celery, parsley, pimiento and seasonings with mayonnaise and mustard. Fold gently into potatoes and stir as little as possible. (Additional mayonnaise may be added as needed.) Sprinkle with paprika; garnish with olives and parsley sprigs.

RAW SPINACH SALAD

Serves 6–8

½ pound raw spinach
¼ cup chopped green bell pepper
½ cup sweet onion rings
1 ½ tablespoons lemon juice
1 ½ tablespoons salad oil
¼ teaspoon tarragon
½ teaspoon salt
⅛ teaspoon pepper
2 hard-boiled eggs, sliced
6 anchovy filets

Wash spinach and drain on paper towels to absorb excess water. Tear or cut leaves into bite-sized pieces and put in a salad bowl. Add bell pepper, onion rings, lemon juice, oil, tarragon, salt, and pepper. Toss lightly. Garnish with egg slices and anchovies.

SLICED TOMATOES WITH BASIL

Serves 6–8

3 tomatoes
10 to 12 leaves fresh basil
1 tablespoon olive oil
1 tablespoon wine vinegar
Salt, pepper, garlic salt to taste
Red onion rings (optional)

The essential ingredient in this recipe is the fresh basil. If you have none on hand, then skip the recipe. If desired, the basil and onions can be chopped.

Place tomato slices in over-lapping manner on a platter. Garnish with basil. Sprinkle with oil, vinegar, and seasonings. Add onion rings, if desired.

TOMATOES STUFFED WITH CUCUMBERS

Serves 6

6 ripe tomatoes
Several lettuce leaves
2 cucumbers
Salt, pepper to taste

Dressing:
½ cup sour cream
1 tablespoon lemon juice
1 tablespoon vinegar
½ teaspoon salt
⅛ teaspoon white pepper
½ teaspoon prepared mustard
2 teaspoons chopped parsley

Scald tomatoes so that skins can be easily removed. Cut a slice from the top of each peeled tomato and with a small spoon, scoop out the centers. Place on lettuce beds. Peel cucumbers, dice, and season with salt and pepper and set aside. Mix dressing by adding all ingredients to the sour cream and blending well. Add cucumbers to dressing mix and stir well. Fill tomato cups with cucumber mixture and sprinkle each cup with parsley.

To peel tomatoes easily, dip into boiling water 10 to 15 seconds, then remove and peel. If peel does not come off easily, dip into water a few seconds more, then peel.

WALDORF SALAD

Serves 4–6

1 cup diced celery
1 cup diced red apples, unpeeled
½ cup walnut or pecan meats
¾ cup mayonnaise
Several lettuce leaves

Combine celery, apples, nuts, and mayonnaise together, mixing well. Serve on a bed of lettuce leaves.

TOMATOES STUFFED WITH FISH

Serves 4

Perfect served on a warm day with a glass of Sebastiani Chardonnay.

4 medium tomatoes, peeled
1 cup shrimp, crab, or tuna
1 cup finely chopped tender celery stalks and leaves
2 to 3 green onions, finely chopped
1 teaspoon white vinegar
½ teaspoon salt
⅛ teaspoon pepper
¼ cup mayonnaise
2 teaspoons lemon juice
Beau monde seasoning
Salt
White pepper
Several lettuce leaves
Paprika
Parsley sprigs

Quarter peeled tomatoes, but do not cut entirely through. Add fish to celery and onion and mix well. Then add vinegar, salt, pepper, mayonnaise, and lemon juice. Sprinkle tomatoes with beau monde seasoning, salt, and white pepper and place on bed of lettuce leaves. Spoon fish mixture over tomatoes, dot with mayonnaise, sprinkle with paprika, and top with a sprig of parsley.

SOUR CREAM FRUIT SALAD

Serves 6

1 pint sour cream
1 can mandarin oranges
1 can pineapple tidbits
1 cup shredded coconut
¾ package miniature marshmallows

Combine all ingredients together and chill. If left to stand overnight, the flavor will be improved greatly.

TUNA SALAD

Serves 6

1 head romaine lettuce
1 red onion, sliced or chopped
1 small clove garlic, pressed
1 small can tuna, undrained
Vinegar, salt, pepper to taste

Break lettuce leaves into bite-sized pieces. Add remaining ingredients and toss lightly. Season to taste. Additional oil may be added, if desired.

WATERCRESS SALAD

Serves 6–8

2 large bunches watercress
3 tablespoons olive oil
2 tablespoons wine vinegar
Juice of ½ lemon
Few sliced water chestnuts (optional)
Salt, pepper to taste

Wash watercress and dry leaves thoroughly. Place leaves in salad bowl, sprinkle with salt and pepper, and chill well. Just prior to serving, mix oil, vinegar, and lemon juice together and sprinkle over watercress. Add water chestnuts and toss lightly.

WATERCRESS DRESSING

Makes about 1 ½ cups

½ cup watercress leaves
1 clove garlic, minced
1 cup mayonnaise
2 teaspoons lemon juice
Salt, pepper to taste

Chop watercress and garlic together until very fine. Stir into mayonnaise and lemon juice. Season to taste with salt and pepper. Chill. Serve over wedges of head lettuce.

CASSEROLES

Mushroom Torta, page 185

EASY BAKED BEANS

Serves 4

We recommend serving a Sebastiani Zinfandel with this dish.

2 slices bacon, cut into 1 inch pieces
½ onion, chopped
1 clove garlic, chopped or pressed
1 can (16 ounces) solid pack tomatoes, mashed
⅔ cup Sebastiani Chardonnay, or other dry, white wine
1 can (27 ounces) red kidney beans, drained
Salt, pepper to taste

Fry bacon, not too crisp, and pour out excess grease from pan. Sauté onion with bacon, adding salt, and pepper to taste. Then add garlic, tomatoes, and wine. Cover and simmer for 30 minutes. Add beans and transfer to a casserole dish. Bake uncovered in 350 degree oven for 30 minutes.

BEAN MUSHROOM CASSEROLE

Serves 4–6

1 can French-style green beans
1 can cream of mushroom soup, undiluted
1 package frozen French fried onions

Place the beans in a buttered casserole dish. Spoon soup over beans, making a smooth layer. Place onions evenly over this. Bake in a moderately hot oven (320 degrees) for 30 to 40 minutes, until hot and bubbly.

CHICKEN CASSEROLE

Serves 8

Try a Sebastiani Chardonnay with this casserole.

3 cups cooked boneless chicken, cut into pieces
1 can (10 ½ ounces) cream of chicken soup, undiluted
1 tablespoon lemon juice
¾ cup mayonnaise
1 cup diced celery
2 teaspoons minced onion
½ cup chopped walnuts
½ teaspoon salt
¼ teaspoon pepper
3 hard-boiled eggs, thinly sliced
4 tablespoons Sebastiani Chardonnay, or other dry, white wine
4 tablespoons cooked rice
1 cup sliced mushrooms
Few dashes Worcestershire sauce
2 cups crushed potato chips
Paprika

Mix all ingredients, except potato chips, and paprika, together in a large bowl. Pour into a greased casserole dish. Sprinkle with paprika and top with potato chips. Bake 20 minutes at 450 degrees.

CHEESE CORN SOUFFLÉ

Serves 4-6

½ teaspoon salt
3 eggs, separated
1 can (8 ¾ ounces) cream style corn
1 tablespoon chopped green onions
¼ cup Sebastiani Chardonnay, or other dry, white wine
1 tablespoon quick-cooking tapioca
Dash Tabasco sauce
1 cup shredded processed American cheese

Add salt to egg whites and beat until stiff. With same beater, beat yolks slightly. Combine corn, onion, wine, tapioca, and Tabasco sauce in a small saucepan. Heat to boiling, stirring constantly. Remove from heat and stir into beaten egg yolks. Add cheese and mix well; then fold in egg whites. Turn into a 1-quart baking dish and bake at 350 degrees for 45 minutes until well-puffed and browned on top. Serve at once from baking dish.

MAMIE'S HASH

1 onion, chopped
1 or 2 slices bacon, cut into small pieces
2 cups cooked ham or corned beef, ground or chopped
1 ½ cups cubed raw potatoes
1 clove garlic
⅔ cup tomato sauce
4 tablespoons Sebastiani Chardonnay, or other dry, white wine
Salt, pepper to taste

Sauté onion with bacon, but do not overcook. Add remaining ingredients and pour into a greased casserole dish. Bake 45 minutes at 350 degrees.

MUSHROOM TORTA

Serves 6–8

This torta can be made ahead of serving time and refrigerated until ready for baking. Let stand at room temperature 30 minutes before placing into oven. Can be served hot or cold.

3 cups boiled mushrooms, drained and chopped
¼ cup chopped parsley
4 cloves garlic, pressed
3 medium onions, chopped
2 teaspoons basil
1 teaspoon oregano
2 teaspoons marjoram
½ teaspoon sage
¼ cup olive oil
6 whole eggs
2 teaspoons salt
½ teaspoon pepper
½ teaspoon paprika
1 ½ cups grated Parmesan cheese
¾ cup bread crumbs

Sauté mushrooms, parsley, garlic, onions, and spices in oil until onion is transparent. Remove from stove and set aside. Whip eggs with fork in large bowl with salt, pepper, and paprika. Add reserved mushroom mixture and stir so that egg does not cook. Add cheese and stir; then add bread crumbs, a small amount at a time, until mixture is the consistency of dressing. Grease a baking dish and sprinkle with bread crumbs, shaking out excess. Pour mixture into dish, but do not pack. Sprinkle a little oil and bread crumbs on top. Bake at 350 degrees for 30 minutes until light brown. Do not overbake.

Spinach Casserole, on opposite page

SHELLFISH CASSEROLE

Serves 8

1 cup vegetable or tomato juice
1 cup mayonnaise
1 can crabmeat or 1 cup fresh crab
1 can shrimp or 1 cup fresh shrimp
2 cups cooked rice
⅓ cup chopped green bell pepper
2 tablespoons butter
1 cup bread crumbs
½ cup slivered almonds
Salt, pepper to taste

Combine juice and mayonnaise and mix well. Stir in crab, shrimp, rice, and bell pepper. Salt and pepper to taste. Mix until ingredients are well-distributed. Pour into a greased 2-quart casserole dish. In a small pan, melt butter and add bread crumbs and almonds. Mix with fork until all crumbs are coated with butter. Pour over casserole. Bake at 375 degrees for about 30 minutes.

SPINACH CASSEROLE

Serves 8

2 packages frozen chopped spinach
1 ½ cups sliced fresh mushrooms
1 small onion, chopped
½ cup chopped celery
1 can cream of mushroom soup, undiluted

Defrost and break apart spinach. Sauté mushrooms with onion and celery until all are tender. Combine onion-celery sauté with spinach and soup in a greased casserole dish. Bake at 375 degrees for 30 minutes.

TAMALE PIE

1 onion, chopped
2 cloves garlic, chopped
2 tablespoons olive oil
2 tablespoons butter
1 pound ground round
½ pound ground pork
1 can pitted olives with liquid
1 can creamed corn
1 can (8 ounces) tomato sauce
¾ cup polenta
1 green pepper, chopped
¾ cup milk
2 to 3 eggs, slightly beaten
2 to 3 tablespoons chili powder
1 cup water
Salt, pepper to taste

Saute onion and garlic lightly in oil and butter. Add meats, season with salt and pepper, and keep stirring. Add corn, olives, 4 to 5 tablespoons olive liquid, and tomato sauce. Stir well, then add polenta, and cook together. Add green pepper and salt and pepper to taste once again. Add milk, eggs, chili powder, and water, mix well. Place in a greased casserole dish and bake 30 to 40 minutes at 300 degrees.

SYLVIA'S KITCHEN

Incorporating its rich winemaking history, the culinary talents of the late family matriarch, Sylvia Sebastiani and her daughter Mary Ann Sebastiani Cuneo, Sebastiani created a line of gourmet food products. The family's Italian heritage and traditions are very present in these products, and they utilize the wealth of fresh ingredients available in Sonoma County. "These foods combine our family's rich heritage and geography, from old-world Italy to new-world Sonoma. Many of the products are based on the dishes in the cookbook *Mangiamo: The Sebastiani Family Cookbook*, my mother's collection of family recipes and traditions," says Mary Ann Sebastiani Cuneo.

The specialty foods, packaged under the "Sylvia's Kitchen" brand, were developed by Sebastiani to accompany their wines, many of which are key ingredients in the recipes, such as Fig Orange Tapenade with Chardonnay and Herb Marinade with Pinot Noir (featured in *Wine Spectator*).

The line, exclusive to the winery, also includes Garlic Mustard, Green Olive Tapenade, Hot Peach Balsamic, Lemon Ginger Oil, Pear Blackberry Vinegar, Apple Pear Vinegar, and Old California Dipping oil with sun-dried tomatoes.

The packaging for Sylvia's Kitchen tells part of the story. The label depicts the family "vine" with its roots anchored in Sylvia's Kitchen and a hang tag with Mary Ann's suggestions for how and where to use these foods. Sylvia would be proud of the way each product is prepared: in the old-world way, step by step, adding ingredients one at a time and allowing for the richness of the flavors to develop.

Zabaglione Classic, page 215 and Wine Cake, page 235

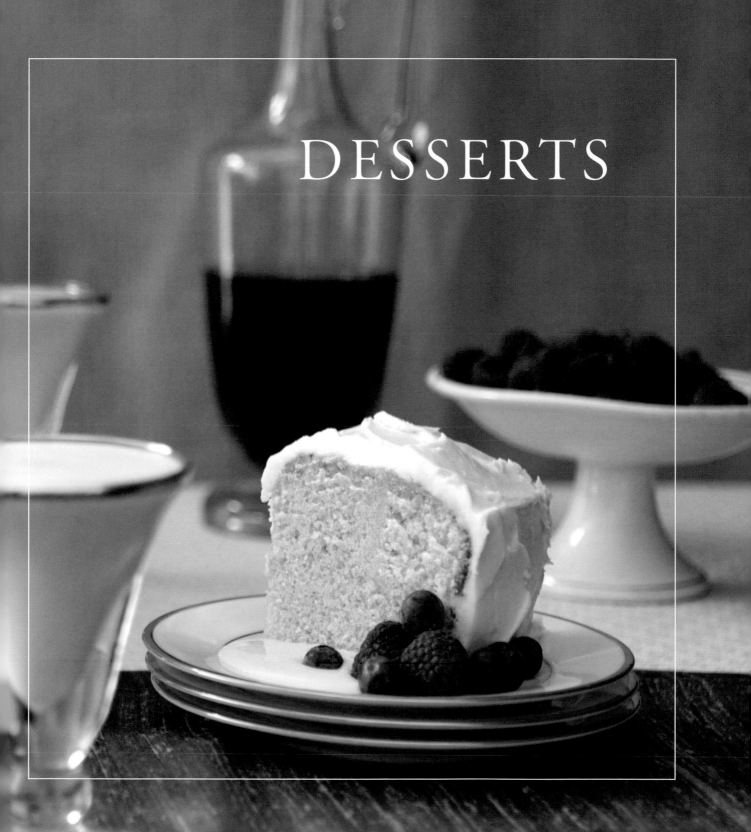

DESSERTS

desserts, cookies, & torte tips

1. To assure proper baking, be sure that your oven thermostat is accurate. To test, simply place an oven thermometer inside oven and check its temperature with that shown on the oven control.

2. Always read recipe thoroughly and make sure you have all ingredients in their sufficient amounts on hand.

3. Butter gives all desserts a better flavor and texture, more so than any other shortening. Pure vanilla is also preferred to imitation vanilla.

4. If a piece of egg shell drops into a bowl, it can easily be removed by using a piece of eggshell as a spoon. And when separating eggs, if a bit of yolk is in the whites, use this same method to get the yolk out.

5. Be accurate in measuring all ingredients and be sure to use only the specified amount on each.

6. Check that you have proper size baking tins on hand and that they are always clean.

7. Strawberries are delicious when served with any wine or sparkling wine. For an extra touch, I like to rinse the berries, after they are stemmed, with a white table wine, instead of washing them with water. When this is done, no watery flavor results in the berries.

8. If you like to make a great many cookies for gifts, especially at Christmas time, you will save time and fuel if you buy two or more racks for your oven. You will thus be able to bake four pans of cookies at a time and cut your baking time in half.

9. When baking many cookies, use more pans than racks in oven so that rotation is possible. Take the pan on the top rack out of the oven, move all other pans up one rack, and place a new pan in on the bottom rack. This helps eliminate burning the bottom of the cookies and keeps them from being too brown on top.

APRICOT BARS

1 ½ cups flour
1 teaspoon baking powder
1 cup brown sugar
1 ½ cups quick oats
¾ cup butter
1 pint apricot jam

Mix flour, baking powder, sugar, and oats together. Mix well, then cut in butter until texture of pie crust. In greased pan (8 x 13), put two-thirds of the mixture and pat firm. Spread jam over this. Put the rest of the mixture on top. Bake at 325 degrees for 45 minutes. Cool and cut into squares, lifting out with a spatula.

BAKED APPLES

Serves 4

1 cup Sebastiani Zinfandel, or other dry, red wine
⅔ cup sugar
¼ cup cinnamon "red hots" (optional)
1 tablespoon lemon juice
4 apples, peeled
4 teaspoons sour cream

Chopped nuts may also be added to the center of apples before baking, if desired.

Mix together wine, sugar, "red hots," and lemon juice. Pour over apples and bake at 350 degrees for 50 minutes. Serve with a teaspoon of sour cream over each apple.

BRANDY PINEAPPLES

Serves 4

4 macaroons
1 can (20 ounces) pineapple chunks, reserve juice
4 jiggers brandy
½ cup slivered almonds

Place 1 macaroon at bottom of each sherbet glass. Spoon pineapple chunks into each glass and cover with 1 tablespoon pineapple juice. Pour 1 jigger brandy into each glass and top with slivered almonds. Chill for at least 2 hours before serving.

BROWN SUGAR APPLE CRISP

6 apples, peeled and sliced
6 tablespoons water
½ cup sugar
1 teaspoon cinnamon
1 teaspoon nutmeg
¼ cup butter
1 cup brown sugar
1 cup flour
½ pint whipping cream

Place apples in buttered baking dish. Cover with water, sugar, and spices. Work butter, brown sugar, and flour together until the consistency of cornmeal. Crumble this mixture on top of apples and sprinkle with more spices, as desired. Bake 30 minutes at 350 degrees. Serve with whipped cream on top.

For an original twist, make your own macaroons (recipe in this book). They're simple, quick, and very delicious.

Pair this dessert with a Sebastiani Symphony.

BURNED PEACHES

Serves 6

6 canned peach halves, reserve syrup
½ cup sugar
2 tablespoons brown sugar
2 tablespoons cinnamon
2 tablespoons lemon juice
6 teaspoons currant jelly
6 teaspoons brandy

Add reserved syrup from peaches with sugar and brown sugar. Boil for 25 minutes or until thick. Place peach halves in Pyrex baking dish. Sprinkle with cinnamon and lemon juice. Place 1 teaspoon jelly in center of each half. Pour peach syrup around and bake for 20 minutes at 350 degrees. Pour over brandy just before serving, set flame, and burn.

STEAMED CARROT PUDDING

1 cup grated raw carrots
1 cup grated potatoes
1 cup sugar
½ cup butter
2 eggs
1 cup flour
1 teaspoon baking soda
1 teaspoon cloves
1 teaspoon cinnamon
½ teaspoon nutmeg
Salt to taste
½ cup raisins
½ cup currants
½ cup walnuts

Mix carrots, potatoes, sugar, and butter. Add eggs, flour and soda, blending well. Add spices and after well-blended, add raisins, currants, and walnuts. Put into steamer, filled about ⅔ full with water. Cover and steam in water for 2 hours. Serve with Hard Sauce (see recipe in this book).

CHESS TARTS

Makes 3 dozen

Pastry for 1 pie crust (see recipe on page 237)
1 scant cup sugar
½ cup butter, softened
1 or 2 eggs
½ cup currants
1 cup chopped nuts
1 cup shredded coconut
1 teaspoon vanilla
Glazed fruits (optional)

Line small muffin tins with pastry. With electric mixer, cream sugar and butter. Add remaining ingredients and mix well. Fill pastry shells and bake at 375 degrees for 20 minutes.

STEAMED CRANBERRY PUDDING

2 tablespoons butter
¾ cup sugar
1 egg, beaten
2 cups flour
4 teaspoons baking powder
½ teaspoon salt
1 cup milk
3 ⅓ tablespoons orange juice
½ teaspoon grated orange rind
1 cup raw cranberries, cut into pieces

Butter Sauce:
½ cup sugar
½ cup heavy cream
½ cup butter

Cream butter and sugar; add egg. Sift flour, baking powder, and salt. Add this alternately with milk to creamed mixture. Add orange juice and rind. Mix well. Then add cranberries. Put into steamer about two-thirds full with water and steam for 2 hours.

Prepare sauce by mixing sugar, cream, and butter. Stir together and cook over boiling water for 15 minutes. Use as topping for pudding.

MACAROON TRIFLE

¼ pound almond macaroons
¼ pound ladyfingers
½ cup raspberry jam
Custard Sauce (below)
¼ cup Sebastiani Symphony, or other sweet, white wine
¼ cup brandy
Maraschino cherries
½ pint whipping cream

Custard Sauce:
2 tablespoons cornstarch
2 cups milk
3 tablespoons sugar
3 egg yolks
3 tablespoons water

Break macaroons and ladyfingers in two and mix together. Line a small bowl (about 6 cup size) with part of the jam. Add part of the cakes to lining of the bowl. Spread with remaining jam.

Make custard sauce by blending cornstarch with ½ cup cold milk. Heat the remaining 1 ½ cups milk in double boiler, then stir in cornstarch mixture. Beat together sugar, egg yolks, and water, stirring constantly, and add milk mixture. Cook 5 to 10 minutes to a thin custard consistency. Let cool. Add wine and brandy to cooled custard sauce and whip all three together. Add custard sauce to the remainder of the cakes and fill the bowl. Cover and refrigerate overnight. Just before serving, decorate with cherries and whipped cream.

MACAROONS

Makes 3 dozen

3 egg whites
1 can (8 ounces) almond paste
1 cup sugar

Beat egg whites. Cut almond paste into small pieces and add to egg whites along with sugar. Mix until smooth and there are no lumps. Drop by rounded teaspoonfuls onto brown paper placed on top of cookie sheet. Bake in 325 degree oven for about 30 minutes. Allow to cool, then wet back of paper to remove macaroons easily.

ORANGE SHERRY CREAM

½ cup sugar
1 envelope unflavored gelatin
¼ teaspoon salt
2 teaspoons grated orange rind
⅓ cup orange juice
3 eggs, separated
1 tablespoon fresh lemon juice
½ cup dry sherry
1 cup whipping cream
1 package (3 ounces) lady fingers
1 package (10 ounces) frozen raspberries, thawed

Combine sugar, gelatin, salt, and orange rind in top of double boiler. Stir in orange juice and lightly beaten egg yolks. Place over hot water; cook, stirring frequently, until mixture thickens, about 10 to 15 minutes. Remove from heat; stir in lemon juice and sherry. Cool until slightly thickened. Beat egg whites until stiff; then whip cream. Fold egg whites and cream into gelatin mixture. Line a 8- or 9-inch spring form pan with lady fingers with tips cut off. Carefully pour gelatin mixture into pan. Chill until firm. Cut into wedges and serve with raspberries.

PANETTONE

1 cup butter, softened
1 ½ cups sugar
4 eggs
1 cup milk
1 tablespoon vanilla
1 tablespoon brandy
1 tablespoon rum
1 tablespoon anise (optional)
1 tablespoon grated lemon peel
4 cups flour
4 teaspoons baking powder
1 teaspoon salt
1 cup raisins
½ cup chopped citron
½ cup chopped glazed cherries
½ cup pine nuts

Cream butter and sugar; then add eggs one at a time, beating well after each addition. Add milk, vanilla, brandy, rum, anise, and lemon peel and blend well. Sift flour, baking powder, and salt together and gradually add to creamed mixture. Fold in raisins, citron, cherries, and nuts until well-blended. Pour into a greased and floured 9-inch angel food pan and bake at 350 degrees for about 1 hour or until panettone is done when tested with a toothpick.

PEACHES IN WINE SAUCE

Serves 8

Canned peaches may be used instead of fresh peaches.

4 large fresh peaches
¾ cup sugar
2 cups water
1 teaspoon vanilla
2 egg yolks
¼ teaspoon salt
¾ cup sifted powdered sugar
⅓ cup Sebastiani Symphony, or other sweet, white wine
1 cup whipping cream
Nutmeg

Peel, pit, and halve peaches. Boil sugar and water. Add peaches. Simmer 5 to 10 minutes until peaches are tender. Add vanilla and chill until ready to serve. Beat egg yolks and salt until thick and lemon-colored. Add powdered sugar gradually and beat until thick. Add wine. Whip cream and fold into egg yolk mixture. Spoon over the peaches and sprinkle with nutmeg.

PERSIMMON PUDDING

2 cups persimmon pulp
3 eggs
1 ¼ cups sugar
1 ½ cups flour
1 teaspoon baking powder
1 teaspoon baking soda
½ teaspoon salt
½ cup melted butter
1 teaspoon vanilla
2 ½ cups milk
2 teaspoons cinnamon
1 teaspoon ginger (optional)
½ teaspoon nutmeg
½ cup raisins
½ cup chopped walnuts

Combine all ingredients together and mix well. Bake in a greased 9 x 9 baking dish for 1 hour at 325 degrees until firm. Top with Hard Sauce (see recipe on page 249) before serving.

RICE PUDDING

Serves 8–10

6 eggs
1 quart milk
Pinch of salt
1 cup sugar
1 teaspoon vanilla
2 cups rice, cooked
½ cup currants

Put eggs, milk, salt, and sugar together and beat well. Add vanilla, rice, and currants and mix well. Place in a baking dish. Place this dish in a shallow pan with water and bake in a 300 degree oven for 1 hour.

STRAWBERRY SHORTCAKE

Serves 6

2 ½ cups Bisquick
3 tablespoons butter
3 tablespoons sugar
½ cup half-and-half
2 baskets strawberries
½ pint whipping cream

Mix Bisquick, butter, sugar, and cream together, forming a soft dough. Knead 8 to 10 times on a lightly-floured board and roll 1/2 inch thick. Cut with a floured 3 inch cutter and bake on ungreased baking sheet in 450 degree oven for 10 minutes. Wash, hull, and halve berries. Add desired amount of sugar to sweeten. Split warm shortcakes in two and spoon berries between and over layers. Top with whipped cream.

BON BONS

Makes about 4 dozen

Enjoy this chocolate treat with a Sebastiani Pinot Noir.

2 egg whites
Pinch cream of tartar
1 cup sugar
½ teaspoon vanilla
¼ teaspoon green food coloring
1 package (6 ounces) mint-flavored chocolate chips

Preheat oven to 350 degrees. Stiffly beat egg whites with cream of tartar. Slowly add sugar, vanilla, and food coloring. Fold in chocolate chips. (Add more food coloring if necessary.) Drop by tablespoonfuls onto foil covered cookie sheets. Turn off oven, place cookie sheets in, and leave overnight. Remove the next morning. DO NOT PEEK!

BRANDY BALLS

Makes about 4 dozen

2 tablespoons cocoa
1 cup powdered sugar
⅓ cup brandy
2 tablespoons corn syrup
2 cups finely crushed vanilla wafers
1 cup chopped walnuts or pecans
Granulated sugar

Sift together cocoa and sugar. Combine and stir in brandy and corn syrup. Combine crushed wafers and nuts. Add chocolate mixture and mix well. Form into 1 inch balls and roll in sugar. Let sit in covered container several days.

BUGIE (SWEET PASTRY)

2 cups flour
2 to 3 eggs
2 tablespoons rum
1 tablespoon sugar
⅛ teaspoon salt
Oil for deep frying
Powdered sugar

Place flour in a bowl and make a well in the center. Add eggs, rum, sugar, and salt. Mix ingredients until well-blended and dough can be gathered into a rough ball. Sprinkle a little flour on a board or pastry cloth and knead for 10 minutes until dough is smooth and shiny. Refrigerate for 1 hour. Heat 3 to 4 inches oil in a deep fryer or deep, heavy saucepan. Roll out chilled dough, about one-fourth at a time, until paper thin. Cut with a sharp knife into strips 6 inches long and ½ inch wide. Tie strips into loose knots and deep fry them 4 or 5 at a time for 1 to 2 minutes until they are delicately brown. With a strainer spoon, transfer bugie to paper towels to drain. Repeat procedure until all dough has been used. Just before serving, sprinkle with powdered sugar.

CRÊPES SUZETTES

Serves 10

6 eggs
1 ½ cups sifted flour
1 ¾ cups milk
½ teaspoon salt
1 ½ tablespoons sugar
½ cube butter, melted

Sauce:
2 oranges
Few drops lemon juice
½ cup brandy
Granulated sugar

Beat eggs, flour, milk, salt, and sugar together. After batter is well-blended, pour in butter and blend well. Let batter stand at least 30 minutes before using. If it becomes too thick on standing, add a teaspoon of water or milk. Drop 2 tablespoons of batter into a well-buttered 6 inch skillet and cook over moderate heat. Fold the thin cake twice after removing from pan.

Sauce:
Extract juice from oranges and set aside. Grind orange rinds and add to orange juice. Add lemon juice and ¼ cup brandy. Pour sauce over crêpes and sprinkle with granulated sugar. Just before serving, pour remaining brandy, heated, over crêpes. Ignite and serve flaming.

These crêpes go well with a Sebastiani Eye of the Swan or Symphony.

GELATIN AND ICE CREAM

Serves 8

1 package strawberry gelatin
1 ¼ cups hot water
1 quart vanilla ice cream
½ pint whipping cream
8 fresh strawberries

Mix gelatin with hot water and chill, but do not let thicken. Cut ice cream into pieces and, with rotary beater, add to gelatin, beating well until all ingredients are combined and smooth. Pour into individual sherbet glasses and chill until firm. Top with whipped cream and a strawberry.

This dessert can also be made with other flavors of gelatin, e.g., orange, raspberry, cherry, etc. The mixture may be poured into a baked pie shell and chilled for a different type of pie entirely.

GINGERBREAD

½ cup butter
1 ½ cups brown sugar, firmly packed
2 ¼ cups dark molasses
10 cups flour
1 ½ teaspoons allspice
1 ½ teaspoons cinnamon
2 ½ teaspoons ginger
1 ½ teaspoons salt
1 cup cold water
1 tablespoon baking soda

Cream butter and sugar together until light and fluffy. Stir in molasses. Sift flour with spices and salt and add to creamed mixture alternately with ¾ cup water. Dissolve soda in remaining ¼ cup water and stir soda into dough. Chill before rolling out and cutting into whatever shapes you desire. Bake 20 minutes in 325 degree oven and cool. Decorate as you please.

It has long been a tradition in our home to have a gingerbread party every year at Christmas time. Even though some "children" are grown and married, they return to participate along with the grandchildren. This recipe makes quite a large amount of dough, so there is plenty for each child to be creative with decorating. Gingerbread freezes quite well and we always keep some gingerbread men in the freezer and pass them out to children when they come to visit each year.

AUNT MARY'S ITALIAN BISCOTTI

Makes about 4 dozen

½ cup butter
¾ cup sugar
3 eggs
½ teaspoon vanilla
3 cups flour
3 teaspoons baking powder
½ teaspoon salt
2 tablespoons grated lemon peel
2 tablespoons grated orange peel
1 tablespoon anise seed
1 cup chopped almonds

Cream butter and sugar, then add eggs one at a time, beating well after each addition. Add vanilla. Sift together flour, baking powder, and salt and add slowly to creamed mixture. Stir in lemon and orange peels, anise seed, and nuts and blend well. Divide dough into 3 parts and shape each part into a long roll about 1 ½ inches in diameter. Place rolls onto cookie sheet several inches apart and flatten rolls somewhat. Bake at 350 degrees for 15 minutes. Then remove from oven and slice rolls crosswise ¾ inches thick. Lay cut side down on cookie sheet, return to oven, and bake an additional 15 minutes.

LACE CURTAIN COOKIES

Makes about 3 dozen

1 cup flour
1 cup chopped nuts
1 cup corn syrup
1 cup shortening
1 cup brown sugar

Blend flour and nuts and set aside. Bring corn syrup, shortening, and sugar to a boil over medium heat, stirring constantly. Remove from heat and gradually stir in flour and nuts. Drop by level teaspoonfuls on lightly greased baking sheet about 3 inches apart. Bake in 375 degree oven for 5 minutes. Let stand 5 minutes before removing from baking sheet.

This recipe makes a biscotti which is not very sweet in the traditional manner of Italian baking. If you prefer things sweet, increase the amount of sugar to 1 full cup. For something really different, try dunking these biscotti in a glass of Sebastiani Pinot Noir, or enjoy with a Sebastiani Symphony.

Aunt Mary's Italian Biscotti, page 207

Pair these cookies with a Sebastiani Chardonnay.

MERINGUE COOKIES

Makes 3 dozen

3 egg whites
1 ½ cups sugar
3 teaspoons baking powder
Tiny colored candies

Beat egg whites until stiff. Add ⅔ of the sugar gradually. Add remaining sugar with baking powder. Put through pastry decorating tube and bake on brown paper at 350 degrees for 6 minutes. Top with tiny candies.

PERSIMMON COOKIES

Makes 3 dozen

½ cup shortening
1 cup sugar
1 egg
1 cup persimmon pulp
½ teaspoon cinnamon
½ teaspoon nutmeg
½ teaspoon cloves
½ teaspoon salt
½ teaspoon baking soda
2 cups flour
1 cup raisins
1 cup chopped nuts

Cream shortening and add sugar slowly. Then add egg and beat well. Add persimmon pulp, spices, salt, baking soda, and flour. Fold in raisins and nuts. Drop by teaspoonfuls onto greased cookie sheet. Bake in 350 degree oven for 10 to 15 minutes.

SALLY'S RANCH COOKIES

Makes 16 dozen

2 cups shortening
2 cups white sugar
2 cups brown sugar
4 eggs
2 teaspoons vanilla
4 tablespoons water
4 cups flour
2 teaspoons soda
2 teaspoons baking powder
1 teaspoon salt
4 cups Quick Oats
4 cups Rice Krispies
1 cup chopped walnuts (optional)

Cream shortening well, add white sugar, and brown sugar slowly until thoroughly blended. Add eggs, one at a time, and vanilla, and beat well. Add water. Sift flour, then measure and combine with soda, baking powder and salt and add to creamed mixture. Fold in oats and Rice Krispies, and nuts, if desired. Bake for 10 to 15 minutes at 350 degrees.

NUTTY NOUGATS

1 cup butter
¼ cup powdered sugar
½ teaspoon salt
1 teaspoon vanilla
1 tablespoon water
2 cups sifted enriched flour
1 cup chopped pecans or walnuts

Cream butter and powdered sugar thoroughly. Add salt, vanilla, water, and flour and blend well. Add nuts. Form into small balls or rolls the size of a finger. Bake on ungreased cookie sheet in 300 degree oven for about 15 minutes.

RAISIN CRISPIES

Makes about a dozen small cookies

¾ cup raisins
½ cup shortening
¼ cup water
I teaspoon vanilla
I cup brown sugar
¾ cup flour
½ teaspoon salt
½ teaspoon baking soda
½ teaspoon cinnamon
I ½ cups rolled oats (quick type), uncooked

Rinse and drain raisins. Combine with shortening and water and heat only until shortening melts, stirring constantly. Let cool. Stir in vanilla and sugar. Sift flour with salt, baking soda, and cinnamon. Stir into raisin mixture, blending well. Stir in oats. Drop by teaspoonfuls onto greased cookie sheet. Bake at 350 degrees for 10 minutes.

APPLE TORTE

2 ½ cups graham cracker crumbs, about 24 crackers
¼ cup butter
½ teaspoon cinnamon
3 eggs, separated
I can Eagle Brand condensed milk
2 tablespoons lemon juice
I can applesauce
½ pint whipping cream

Blend 2 cups crumbs with butter and cinnamon. Use this to line a greased spring form pan. Beat egg yolks until thick; stir in milk carefully. Alternately mix lemon juice and applesauce into milk and egg yolk mixture. Beat egg whites stiff and fold gently into mixture. Pour into pan and sprinkle with remaining crumbs. Bake at 350 degrees for 50 minutes. Top with whipped cream before serving.

HELEN'S MAPLE NUT TORTE

4 eggs, separated
1 ½ cups maple syrup
½ teaspoon salt
2 envelopes unflavored gelatin
½ cup water
2 cups whipped cream
20 macaroons, dried in a low oven and rolled into crumbs
1 ½ cups chopped nuts
10 to 15 whole macaroons

Beat egg yolks slightly; add maple syrup and salt and cook on top of a double boiler until of custard consistency, stirring frequently. Soften gelatin in water, add to hot maple custard, and stir until dissolved. Cool custard, then add whipped cream, macaroon crumbs, and nuts. Fold in stiffly-beaten egg whites. Pour into a 10-inch spring form pan that has been lined with whole macaroons. Chill overnight and before unmolding for serving, top with more whipped cream and nuts, if desired.

NONI VERA'S TORTE

Makes 2 tortes

2 cups cooked Swiss chard, chopped or 3 frozen packages chard
1 onion, chopped
2 cloves garlic, finely chopped
1 teaspoon parsley
¼ teaspoon thyme
½ cup bread crumbs
1 cup raisins, dark or white
½ cup pine nuts
½ cup grated Parmesan cheese
½ cup sugar
1 cup half-and-half
6 eggs
1 teaspoon salt

This dish is often served after the main course and before dessert. My grandmother's dish was served in our home as a Christmas tradition.

More sugar may be added if you like. My family doesn't like this too sweet, but maybe yours will, so cook to please their tastes. Sometimes I add a little pork sausage to the torte mixture (¼ cup meat, finely chopped, and sautéed, is sufficient).

recipe continued on next page

½ teaspoon pepper
Dash of allspice or nutmeg

Crust:
3 cups flour
2 teaspoons baking powder
3 tablespoons sugar
¼ teaspoon salt
¼ cup rum
4 eggs
5 tablespoons butter, melted
¼ cup half-and-half
¼ cup chopped walnuts (optional)
1 square chocolate, grated
Granulated sugar

Cook chard; cool, drain, and squeeze dry. Sauté onion and garlic; sprinkle in parsley and thyme. Combine with bread crumbs and chard and mix well. Add raisins, pine nuts, cheese, sugar, half-and-half, eggs, seasonings, and spices. Mix well.

Crust:
Combine all ingredients except walnuts, chocolate, and granulated sugar and mix well until crust is of kneading consistency. Knead a few times. Use very little flour when rolling dough to size. Oil two pie tins and line with dough. Be sure to roll out dough big enough, as it has an elastic quality. Put in filling, making sure dough does not extend over edge of pan. Sprinkle walnuts and chocolate and a little sugar over each torte. Bake at 375 degrees for 20 minutes, then reduce heat to 325 degrees, and bake for an additional 20 minutes.

POPPY SEED TORTE

⅓ cup poppy seeds
¾ cup milk
¾ cup butter
1 ½ cups sugar
1 ½ teaspoons vanilla
2 cups flour
2 ½ teaspoons baking powder
¼ teaspoon salt
4 egg whites

Filling:
½ cup sugar
1 tablespoon constarch
1 ½ cups milk
4 egg yolks, slightly beaten
1 teaspoon vanilla
¼ cup chopped walnuts
⅓ cup powdered sugar

Soak poppy seeds in milk for 1 hour. Cream butter and gradually add sugar, creaming well. Stir in vanilla, poppy seeds, and milk. Sift together flour, baking powder, and salt; stir into creamed mixture. Fold in beaten egg whites. Pour into two well-greased and lightly-floured round cake pans. Bake at 375 degrees for 20 to 25 minutes. Let cool 10 minutes in pans. Remove to racks.

Mix sugar with cornstarch. Combine with milk and egg yolks. Cook and stir until mixture thickens and boils (about 1 minute). Cool slightly, then add vanilla and nuts. Cool thoroughly.

Split each cake into 2 layers. Assemble torte, spreading the filling between the layers. Sift powdered sugar over top. Chill 2 to 3 hours before serving.

SCHAUM TORTE (MERINGUE)

6 egg whites
2 cups granulated sugar
2 teaspoons vinegar
1 teaspoon vanilla
½ pint whipping cream, sweetened
Berries or fruit of your choice

Beat egg whites until stiff. Beat in sugar 2 teaspoons at a time, beating thoroughly after each addition. Add vinegar and vanilla, blending well. Pour into greased spring form pan and bake at 250 degrees for 1 hour. Turn off oven and let torte cool in oven with door open for at least 1 hour. Remove from oven; torte will have a light airy crust from baking. Remove this crust carefully and fill torte with whipped cream and berries or other fruit. Replace crust and serve.

For a variation, use ice cream in place of the whipped cream.

ZABAGLIONE CLASSIC

Makes about 4 servings

6 egg yolks
½ cup sugar
¼ cup Sebastiani Symphony, or other sweet, white wine
Grated rind and juice of 1 lemon
Touch of brandy (optional)

Measure ingredients into top of double boiler and place over boiling water. Beat constantly with a rotary beater until mixture thickens and mounds like whipped cream. Remove from heat. Serve hot or chilled in tall parfait glasses alone or as a topping for sponge cake or canned fruit.

This very old Italian dessert is excellent after a heavy dinner. It is especially nice because it can be made on the spur of the moment.

cake tips

1. When baking cakes, place layer pans in the center of the oven or space them so that even baking is assured.

2. Don't adhere strictly to suggested baking times given in recipes. Always test cakes for doneness. When toothpick comes out clean, the cake is done. Or you can touch the cake lightly on top: if it springs back, it is done; if the impression of your finger remains, bake a few minutes longer.

3. Do not overbake cake or it will be crusty and have a poor texture.

4. If cake has a tendency to stick to the pan, wrap a towel dipped in hot water around the pan after it is removed from the oven. You will be able to remove the cake to a rack in just a few minutes.

5. While cake mixes are popular because they are time-saving and economical, they can never equal a cake produced from scratch using fresh ingredients. If you do use a packaged cake mix, add ¼ cup of any cooking oil to the batter. This will ensure that the cake will stay fresh and keep moist.

6. When using packaged cake mixes, you can improve the cake tremendously if you split the layers and spread with pudding mixes. I usually fill a chocolate cake with chocolate pudding and a white cake with vanilla or lemon pudding. Simply cook pudding according to directions given on pudding package, but decrease amount of milk from 2 cups to 1 ¾ cups. It takes two packages of pudding mix to fill a cake with four layers (2 regular layers, split into halves). After assembling cake, frost with your favorite frosting and serve.

7. Packaged cake mixes can be quite versatile if you use a little creativity. For a banana nutmeg cake, simply mix 1 package of yellow cake mix as directed on package, adding ⅛ teaspoon baking soda and ½ teaspoon nutmeg and substituting 1 cup mashed bananas for half of the water called for in the recipe. After baking, fill and frost with the frosting of your choice.

Another variation is to substitute ⅔ cup drained, crushed pineapple for ⅓ of the water needed in a yellow cake mix. Also add 2 teaspoons grated lemon rind to mix before pouring into cake pans. Frost as you wish.

As a general rule, substitute ½ cup of whatever juice or liquid you desire for ½ cup of water called for in the directions given on the package of cake mix. This will give your cakes a different flavor without having to bake from scratch.

ANGEL CAKE CLOUD

I pint whipping cream
I package frozen strawberries
I cup small marshmallows
I small can crushed pineapple, well-drained
I angel food cake (10 inch)

Beat whipping cream until firm. Fold in fruits and marshmallows. Split angel food cake into 3 layers and put cream mixed with fruit between layers and on top.

WINE ANGEL CAKE

I angel food cake (10 inch)
10 tablespoons Sebastiani Symphony, or other sweet, white wine
2 cups sour cream
I cup sifted powdered sugar
I package (3 ounces) cream cheese

Split angel cake in half horizontally. Sprinkle bottom half with 5 tablespoons of wine, then spread 1 cup of sour cream over it, and dust with 1/2 cup powdered sugar. Replace top of cake. Pour remaining wine over entire cake. Blend cream cheese with remaining sour cream and powdered sugar. Use this as frosting spreading over cake. Chill 4 hours.

BRANDY CAKE

1 ½ cups seedless raisins
1 ½ cups water
¾ cup butter
1 1/2 cups sugar
2 eggs
2 ¼ cups flour
1 ½ teaspoons baking soda
1 teaspoon baking powder
¾ cup brandy
¾ cup ground nuts
Nutmeg and cinnamon to taste

Frosting:
½ cup butter
1 egg yolk, beaten
1 ½ cups powdered sugar
4 tablespoons brandy

Boil raisins and water together until it yields ¾ cup. Drain and keep water. Cool raisins and chop. Cream butter and add sugar. Beat eggs into this creamed mixture. Sift together flour, soda, and baking powder. Add to the first mixture along with water from the raisins and brandy. Add raisins, nuts, nutmeg, and cinnamon. Bake at 350 degrees for 35 minutes in 2 layer pans.

Frosting:
Cream butter along with egg yolk and sugar. Use brandy to moisten. Spread on cooled cake layers.

BOURBON ICE BOX CAKE

3 packages unflavored gelatin
½ cup cold water
Boiling water
6 eggs, separated
4 tablespoons bourbon
I cup sugar
I tablespoon lemon juice
I pint whipping cream
2 packages lady fingers

Soak gelatin in cold water for 5 minutes, then fill with boiling water until there is 1 cup. Stir to dissolve gelatin. Cool until mixture begins to congeal. Beat egg yolks until thick and lemon-colored, adding bourbon slowly while beating. Beat in sugar and continue beating until mixture is very light. Add lemon juice. Whip cream and fold in. Beat egg whites stiff and fold in. Line bottom and sides of a spring form mold with lady fingers. Pour filling into mold and let chill several hours or overnight.

AUNT ROSE'S CARROT CAKE

I ¾ cups sugar
I ¼ cups vegetable oil
4 eggs
2 cups flour
2 teaspoons soda
2 teaspoons baking powder
I teaspoon salt
3 cups grated carrots
½ cup shredded coconut
I cup walnuts

Frosting:
I package (8 ounces) cream cheese
2 teaspoons vanilla
¼ cup butter

recipe continued on next page

1 pound package powdered sugar
½ cup crushed pineapple, drained

Grease and flour 3 eight inch layer pans. Cream sugar and oil. Add eggs one at a time and beat thoroughly. Sift together flour, soda, baking powder, and salt. Add to egg mixture. Fold in carrots, coconut, and nuts. Pour into pans and bake at 325 degrees for 30 minutes.

Frosting:
In electric mixer, blend all ingredients together and spread on cooled cake layers.

CHEESE CAKE

1 ¾ cups graham cracker crumbs
¼ to ½ cup nuts
1 ½ teaspoons cinnamon
½ cup butter, melted
3 eggs, well-beaten
2 packages (8 ounces each) cream cheese
1 cup sugar
¼ teaspoon salt
2 teaspoons vanilla
½ teaspoon almond extract
3 cups sour cream

Combine crumbs, nuts, and cinnamon with butter. Line sides and bottom of spring form pan with this mixture. In mixing bowl, combine eggs, cream cheese, sugar, salt, vanilla, and almond extract. Beat until smooth. Blend in sour cream. Pour into pan and bake at 375 degrees for 35 minutes. Cool 4 to 5 hours.

Enjoy this cake with a Sebastiani Chardonnay.

COFFEE CAKE

Serves 8–10

2 ½ cups flour
¾ cup sugar
¼ teaspoon nutmeg
Pinch of salt
1 cup brown sugar
¾ cup oil
1 egg
1 cup buttermilk or sour milk
1 teaspoon baking soda
1 teaspoon baking powder
1 cup chopped nuts (optional)
Cinnamon (optional)

Mix flour, sugar, nutmeg, salt, brown sugar, and oil thoroughly. Save 1/2 cup of this mixture for the topping. Mix egg, milk, baking soda, and baking powder together and add to the flour mixture, stirring well. Pour into a greased and floured 9 x 9 inch pan, then sprinkle with chopped nuts and cinnamon, if desired. Bake at 325 degrees for 45 minutes.

CRAZY CAKE

1 package yellow cake mix
¾ cup oil
¾ cup water
1 package lemon Jello
4 eggs

Frosting:
1 cup powdered sugar
Juice of 1 lemon

In a mixing bowl, blend cake mix, oil, water, and Jello. Add eggs one at a time and beat for 4 minutes. Bake in a greased and floured 9 x 9 inch pan for 40 to 45 minutes at 350 degrees.

recipe continued on next page

Frosting:

Mix powdered sugar and lemon juice thoroughly and spread on hot cake. Serve hot.

DATE CAKE

1 cup pitted dates, cut into sixths
1 cup water
½ teaspoon baking soda
½ cup butter
1 cup sugar
2 eggs
1 ½ cups flour
1 ½ teaspoons baking powder
1 teaspoon cinnamon
1 teaspoon salt
1 teaspoon vanilla
1 ½ cups nut meats, chopped (optional)

Frosting:
1 cup water
½ cup brown sugar
½ cup white sugar
½ cup chopped walnut meats

Place dates in a bowl. Bring water to a boil in saucepan. Add baking soda, stir until dissolved. Pour water over dates and let cool. Cream together butter and sugar. Add eggs one at a time, beating well. Sift flour with baking powder, cinnamon, and salt. Add to creamed mixture alternately with the water poured off from the dates. Beat well after each addition. Stir in dates, vanilla, and nuts. Spread in a well-greased 9-inch square pan. Bake at 350 degrees for 40 minutes.

Frosting:
Boil all ingredients together for 10 minutes. Continue cooking until mixture is thick. Pour over cooled cake.

EASY DEVIL'S FOOD CAKE

5 rounded tablespoons cocoa
⅔ cup water
Pinch of salt
½ cup shortening
2 cups sugar
3 eggs
1 cup sour milk
2 level teaspoons baking soda
3 tablespoons hot water
2 cups flour
1 teaspoon vanilla

Frosting:
½ pint whipping cream
1 tablespoon powdered sugar
1 tablespoon cocoa

Cook cocoa, water, and salt together for 3 minutes. Let cool. Cream shortening and sugar. Add eggs and cocoa mixture. Then add sour milk and mix well. Dissolve baking soda in hot water and add to mixture. Then add flour and vanilla, mixing well. Bake in greased and floured loaf pan at 350 degrees for 40 minutes.

Frosting:
Beat cream until thick. Add powdered sugar and cocoa and mix until well-blended. Spread over cake.

EGYPTIAN CAKE

5 tablespoons chocolate
5 tablespoons boiling water
½ cup butter
1 ½ cups sugar
4 eggs, separated
½ cup milk
1 ¾ cups flour
2 teaspoons baking powder
Pinch of salt
1 teaspoon vanilla

Filling:
2 eggs, separated
Pinch of salt
1 cup finely chopped nuts
5 tablespoons powdered sugar
1 cup whipping cream
1 teaspoon vanilla

Dissolve chocolate in boiling water. Cream butter, adding sugar gradually. Add beaten egg yolks, milk, and blend well. Add chocolate. Mix and sift flour with baking powder and pinch of salt. Add to creamed mixture. Beat egg whites until stiff and flavor with vanilla. Fold egg white-vanilla mixture gently into cake batter. Pour into greased and well-floured cake pans and bake at 350 degrees for 25 to 30 minutes.

Filling:
Beat eggs yolks until creamy and thick. Add salt, nuts, and sugar. Beat egg whites until stiff and fold into egg yolks. Whip cream and pour egg white mixture into it. Flavor with vanilla. If not thick enough, add more powdered sugar. Spread between layers of cooled cake.

ELEGANT CHEESE CAKE

Accompany this cheese cake with a Sebastiani Symphony.

1 ½ cups zwieback crumbs
¼ cup melted butter
4 tablespoons sugar
4 tablespoons finely ground unblanched almonds
2 tablespoons heavy cream
5 eggs
1 cup sugar
1 ½ pounds cottage cheese, put through a sieve
¼ cup flour
½ pint heavy cream
½ teaspoon salt
Juice and rind of 1 lemon
1 can cherry pie filling (optional)

Combine crumbs, butter, sugar, almonds, and cream. Press mixture thickly against the bottom and sides of a well-buttered, 9-inch spring form pan. Beat eggs until thick and lemon-colored. Add sugar gradually, then add cottage cheese, and beat well. Add flour, cream, salt, and lemon. Pour carefully into pan and bake at 325 degrees for 45 minutes, until firm. Turn off heat, open oven door, and let cake cool in the oven. Spread cherry filling over chilled cake before serving, if desired.

FRUIT COCKTAIL CAKE

Makes 6–8

1 cup flour
1 cup sugar
1 teaspoon baking soda
½ teaspoon salt
1 egg, beaten
1 large can fruit cocktail, well-drained
½ cup brown sugar
½ cup chopped nuts
½ pint whipping cream

Combine flour, sugar, baking soda, and salt. Add egg and fruit cocktail. Pour mixture into well-greased, shallow 9-inch square pan. Mix together brown sugar and nuts and pour over cake mixture. Bake at 300 degrees for 1 hour. Serve topped with whipped cream.

GRAHAM CRACKER CAKE

½ cup butter
1 cup sugar
3 eggs, separated
⅔ cup milk
½ teaspoon salt
25 honey-flavored graham crackers
2 ½ teaspoons baking powder
1 cup chopped nuts
1 teaspoon vanilla
1 pint whipping cream

Cream butter and sugar. Add beaten egg yolks, milk, and salt and beat well. Finely crush graham crackers, mix with baking powder, and add to cream mixture. Add ½ cup nuts and vanilla. Fold in stiffly-beaten egg whites. Pour into 2 layer pans, greased, and well-floured. Bake at 350 degrees for 20 to 25 minutes. Let cool. Fill and top with unsweetened whipped cream and sprinkle with remaining ½ cup nuts.

LADY BALTIMORE CAKE

3 cups flour
3 teaspoons baking powder
½ teaspoon salt
½ cup butter
1 ½ cups sugar
½ cup milk
½ cup water
1 teaspoon vanilla
¼ teaspoon almond extract
3 egg whites, stiffly-beaten

Frosting:
½ cup sugar
⅔ cup boiling water
½ teaspoon corn syrup
2 egg whites, stiffly beaten
1 teaspoon vanilla
½ cup chopped raisins
6 figs, chopped
½ cup chopped walnut or pecan meats

Sift flour, baking powder, and salt together and set aside. Cream butter thoroughly and add sugar gradually, creaming until light and fluffy. Add flour mixture alternately with milk and water, a small amount at a time. Beat well after each addition. Continue in this manner until all flour and liquid has been blended. Add vanilla and almond extracts; then fold in egg whites quickly and thoroughly. Bake in 2 greased 9-inch layer pans at 350 degrees for 20 minutes.

Frosting:
Combine sugar, water, and corn syrup. Bring quickly to a boil until a small amount of syrup forms a soft ball in cold water. Pour syrup in a fine stream over egg whites and beat constantly. Add vanilla and beat with a rotary beater 10 to 15 minutes until frosting is of spreading consistency. Add raisins, figs, and nuts and blend well. Fill and frost cooled layers of cake.

ICE BOX CAKE

Serves 12–14

This dessert can easily be made a few days prior to serving and frozen.

2 dozen lady fingers
4 packages vanilla Whip n' Chill
2 cups milk
1 cup Sebastiani Symphony, or other sweet, white wine
1 cup whipping cream
1 can mandarin oranges (optional)

Line a spring form pan, sides and bottom, with lady fingers. Beat Whip n' Chill with milk, then slowly beat in wine. Beat cream until stiff and fold into Whip n' Chill mixture. Spoon into spring form pan. If desired, decorate with mandarin oranges. Chill.

LEMON CHIFFON ICE BOX CAKE

Delicious served with a glass of Sebastiani Chardonnay.

8 eggs, separated
1 ½ cups sugar
Juice from 2 lemons
1 envelope unflavored gelatin
1 cup cold water
½ cup boiling water
1 package (6 ounces) lady fingers (about 3 dozen)
½ pint whipping cream

Beat egg yolks until light in color. Add 1/2 cup sugar and lemon juice. Cook in top of double boiler until thick. Soak gelatin in cold water about 10 minutes. Dissolve in boiling water and add to custard slowly. Beat egg whites until stiff and fold in the remaining sugar. Then fold into custard. Line a spring form pan with lady fingers and pour custard in. Chill overnight and top with whipped cream before serving.

WALNUT CAKE

1 teaspoon soda
1 cup boiling water
1 cup chopped walnuts
½ cup dates, cut up
½ cup raisins
1 cup sugar
1 teaspoon cinnamon
3 tablespoons cocoa
1 cup mayonnaise
1 ¾ cups flour
1 teaspoon salt
1 teaspoon vanilla
Powdered sugar

Dissolve soda in water. Pour over walnuts, dates, and raisins. Let stand. Sift sugar, cinnamon, and cocoa together. Stir in mayonnaise and drained walnuts, dates, and raisins. Blend well. Sift flour and salt together and add to mayonnaise mixture. Add vanilla and mix well. Pour into greased and floured 8 x 13 inch pan and bake at 350 degrees 30 to 40 minutes. Cover with powdered sugar before serving.

MERINGUE CAKE

½ cup butter
1 ½ cups sugar
4 eggs, separated
2 teaspoons vanilla
5 tablespoons milk
1 cup flour
1 teaspoon baking powder
¼ teaspoon salt
¼ teaspoon cream of tartar

Filling:
4 tablespoons sugar
2 tablespoons cornstarch
½ teaspoon salt
2 egg yolks
2 cups milk
½ pint whipping cream
½ teaspoon vanilla
1 cup strawberries

Cream butter and ½ cup sugar. Add 4 egg yolks, well-beaten, and 1 teaspoon vanilla. Add milk alternately to creamed mixture with flour, baking powder, and salt sifted together. Spread batter in thin layers in 2 layer pans, greased, well-floured, and lined with wax paper, also greased and well-floured. Beat egg whites until they peak, then add cream of tartar. Beat in remaining 1 cup sugar slowly and thoroughly. Add remaining 1 teaspoon vanilla, blend well, and spread mixture on top of cake batter. Bake at 325 degrees for 30 minutes.

Filling:
Combine sugar, cornstarch, and salt together. Stir in egg yolks and add milk. Cook over low heat, stirring until thick, and then add vanilla. Remove cakes from pans. Spread filling over 1 layer and place other layer carefully on top. Whip cream and spread over top. Garnish with fresh strawberries, if in season.

PINEAPPLE UPSIDE-DOWN CAKE

¼ cup butter
2 cups brown sugar
1 large can pineapple slices, drained
½ cup maraschino cherries, drained
½ cup chopped walnuts
1 package yellow cake mix
½ pint whipping cream

Melt butter in a deep, heavy iron skillet and spread all around the sides of the skillet. Cover with brown sugar, spreading evenly. Place 1 pineapple slice in the center and cut rest of the slices in half, crosswise. Arrange these in a circle around the center slice like the spokes of a wheel, rounded edges facing one way. Fill spaces with cherries and walnuts. Prepare cake batter as indicated on package. Pour over pineapples, cherries, and walnuts. Bake at 350 degrees for 30 to 40 minutes until firm. Cool only for a couple of minutes. Place serving dish over skillet and turn upside down to remove cake. Let cool and serve with whipped cream.

POWDERED SUGAR POUND CAKE

1 ½ cups butter
1 box powdered sugar
6 eggs
1 teaspoon vanilla
2¾ cups flour

Beat butter in a large bowl. Add sugar and beat until creamy and fluffy. Add eggs one at a time, beating well after each egg. Add vanilla. Sift and measure flour and add gradually to mixture. Bake at 300 degrees in a greased tube pan for 1 ½ hours. Check cake at 1 hour. (This can also be baked in 2 loaf pans; if so, less baking time is required.)

POTATO CAKE

2 cups sugar
⅔ cup butter
4 eggs, beaten
1 cup mashed potatoes
½ cup ground chocolate, dry
½ cup milk
2 cups flour
3 ½ teaspoons baking powder
¼ teaspoon salt
½ teaspoon cloves
1 teaspoon cinnamon
1 teaspoon nutmeg
1 cup chopped walnuts

Frosting:
1 cup butter, softened
1 cup powdered sugar
4 tablespoons ground chocolate, dry
4 tablespoons boiling water
Chopped walnuts (optional)

Grease and flour 2 layer pans. Cream sugar and butter. Mix together eggs, potatoes, chocolate, milk, flour, baking powder, salt, and spices. Add to creamed mixture, then add walnuts lastly. Pour into pans and bake at 350 degrees for 30 minutes.

Frosting:
Cream butter with powdered sugar and chocolate. Add water and beat well with rotary beater until smooth. Spread between cooled cake layers and on top. Garnish with walnuts, if desired.

PRUNE CAKE

½ cup butter
1 cup sugar
2 eggs
1 ½ cups flour
1 teaspoon cinnamon
1 teaspoon cloves
½ teaspoon salt
1 teaspoon soda
2 teaspoons baking powder
1 ½ tablespoons cornstarch
¾ cup sour cream
1 cup chopped stewed prunes
2 tablespoon prune juice
½ cup chopped walnuts

Filling:
2 eggs beaten
1 cup sugar
½ cup sour cream
½ teaspoon salt
1 cup chopped stewed prunes
2 tablespoons butter
½ pint whipping cream

Cream butter and sugar. Add eggs and beat well. Add dry ingredients and sour cream, blending well. Then add prunes and prune juice. Add walnuts last. Pour into 2 greased and well-floured cake pans and bake at 325 degrees for about 30 to 35 minutes.

Filling:
Mix all ingredients, except whipping cream, together in upper part of a double boiler and cook until very thick, stirring frequently. Let cool, then spread between the cooled cake layers. Top with whipped cream before serving.

RUM CAKE

½ cup shortening
2 cups sugar
1 teaspoon vanilla
1 jigger rum
4 eggs
3 cups flour
½ teaspoon salt
½ teaspoon baking powder
½ teaspoon baking soda
1 cup buttermilk

Topping:
1 ½ cups butter
1 cup sugar
1 teaspoon vanilla
1 jigger rum

Cream shortening, sugar, vanilla, and rum together with electric mixer. Add eggs one at a time, beating well. Sift flour, salt, and baking powder together. Add baking soda to buttermilk. Add small amount of flour mixture to creamed mixture, followed by a small amount of buttermilk, mixing well. Continue in this manner until all flour and buttermilk have been added. Grease a tube pan and pour batter into it. Bake at 325 degrees for 1 hour.

Topping:
Melt all ingredients together. Remove cake from oven, leave in pan, and place on large plate. Pour topping over cake and let stand 4 hours before serving.

WINE CAKE

1 package yellow cake mix
¾ cup oil
¾ cup Sebastiani Symphony, also excellent if you use dry sherry
4 eggs
1 package vanilla pudding
¾ teaspoon nutmeg

Frosting:
½ cup butter
1 package powdered sugar
¼ cup cream sherry

In a mixing bowl, place cake mix, oil, and wine. Blend well, then add eggs one at a time, mixing well after each addition. Then add vanilla pudding and nutmeg and beat 4 minutes at medium speed. Bake for 45 minutes at 350 degrees in tube pan, greased and floured.

Frosting:
Cream butter and add powdered sugar gradually. Add sherry and blend well. Spread over cooled cake and serve.

pie tips

1. You will have one less bowl to wash if you mix the pie dough in the pie pan. Just remember to wipe the pan out with a paper towel after removing dough to the rolling board.

2. The dough for pie crust is always much easier to handle if it is chilled for 30 minutes prior to rolling.

3. Brush bottom crust of fruit and berry pies with soft butter and let harden before filling. This prevents the crust from getting soggy.

4. Make apple pies with apple cubes instead of slices. The cubes support the top crust better and they also allow sugar and seasonings to spread through the pie.

5. Baking time for a pumpkin pie can be halved if the filling is readied and set into a pan of boiling water, stirring occasionally. Place pie crust into heated oven for 10 minutes, then pour warm filling into the partially baked crust. Return pie to oven and reduce baking time to half the time indicated in the recipe.

6. If juices from fruit pies bubble over during baking, sprinkle spilled juice with salt to prevent smoke and odor.

7. When pressed for time, instead of making a regulation pie, just make up the filling, pour into custard cups, and top with meringue. Place the cups into the oven and brown the meringue, then cool. This trick can be used only with such fillings as are poured into cooked pastry shells, e.g., lemon, chocolate, butterscotch, and the like.

PIE CRUST

Makes 2 crusts

2 cups flour
1 teaspoon baking powder
Dash of salt
⅔ cup Crisco
5 to 6 tablespoons ice water

Sift flour, baking powder, and salt into a bowl. Add Crisco, cutting into pieces in flour mixture. Add 1 teaspoon water at a time and blend well. Roll quite thick.

ANGEL PIE

Shell:
4 egg whites
½ teaspoon cream of tartar
1 cup sugar

Filling:
4 egg yolks
½ cup sugar
3 tablespoons lemon juice
2 teaspoons grated lemon rind
1 cup whipping cream

Beat egg whites until foamy, then beat in cream of tartar. Gradually add sugar and beat stiff. Spread in a slightly buttered 9-inch pie plate. Bake at 300 degrees for 40 minutes. Let cool while making the filling.

Filling:
Beat egg yolks until thick and lemon-colored. Beat in sugar, lemon juice, and rind. Cook in a double boiler until thick. Cool. Fold in stiffly-whipped cream. Pour into cooled pie shell and chill for 24 hours.

Apple pie tastes even more delicious when served with a glass of Sebastiani Chardonnay.

APPLE PIE

Pastry for 2 pie crusts (see Pie Crust on page 237)
6 medium-sized apples
½ to ⅔ cup sugar
⅛ teaspoon salt
1 tablespoon flour
¼ teaspoon cinnamon
⅛ teaspoon nutmeg
1 tablespoon lemon juice
1 to 2 tablespoons butter
Melted butter

Line pie pan with half the pastry. Peel, core, and cut apples into cubes. Place cubes into a large bowl and add sugar, salt, flour, spices, and lemon juice. Mix ingredients very gently until apple cubes are well-coated. Then pour into pie pan and dot with butter. Cover with top crust and brush melted butter over crust. Bake 10 minutes at 425 degrees, then reduce heat to 350 degrees, and bake for an additional 45 minutes to 1 hour.

APPLESAUCE CREAM PIE

2 tablespoons unflavored gelatin
4 tablespoons water
2 egg yolks, well-beaten
¼ cup sugar
1 tablespoon flour
1 ¼ cups scalded milk
½ teaspoon vanilla
¼ teaspoon salt
2 ½ cups thick, sweetened apple sauce
2 tablespoons lemon juice
1 baked pie shell
1 ½ pints whipping cream (optional)

Soften gelatin in cold water. Combine egg yolks, sugar, and flour and beat thoroughly. Add milk slowly, stirring constantly. Cook over hot water until

recipe continued on next page

thick, stirring frequently. Remove from heat, add gelatin, and let cool. Mix together vanilla, salt, applesauce, and lemon juice. Add to cooled milk mixture carefully. Pour into pie shell and chill. Serve with or without whipped cream.

BLACK BOTTOM PIE

Serve this pie with a Sebastiani Pinot Noir.

Crust:
17 graham crackers
¼ cup sugar
½ cup butter, melted

Filling:
1 envelope unflavored gelatin
¼ cup cold water
4 eggs, separated
2 cups scalded milk
1 cup sugar
1 ½ tablespoons cornstarch
1 ½ squares baking chocolate, melted
2 teaspoons vanilla
¼ teaspoon cream of tartar
½ pint whipping cream
1 square baking chocolate, grated

Crush crackers very fine. Add sugar and butter and mix well. Pat firmly into pie pan to form crust. Bake 12 to 15 minutes at 400 degrees in oven until brown.

Filling:
Mix gelatin in cold water and set aside. Beat egg yolks and slowly add to scalded milk in top of double boiler. Add ½ cup sugar; then add cornstarch mixed with a little cold water and let simmer 20 minutes. Add gelatin mixture and mix well. Remove from heat and take out 1 cup of custard mixture. To this, add chocolate and 1 teaspoon vanilla. Place in pie crust and chill. Beat egg whites, add cream of tartar, then gradually add ½ cup sugar, and 1 teaspoon vanilla, beating slowly. Fold egg white mixture into custard and spread over the chocolate layer of pie. Top with whipped cream and sprinkle with chocolate.

COFFEE SPONGE PIE

1 tablespoon unflavored gelatin
¼ cup cold water
3 eggs, separated
1 cup sugar
1 cup very strong coffee
¼ teaspoon salt
1 teaspoon vanilla
1 baked pie shell (9 inch)
½ pint whipping cream

Soften gelatin in water and set aside. Beat egg yolks until light and lemon-colored; gradually beat in ½ cup sugar. Add coffee slowly, then salt. Place over boiling water and cook 5 minutes, or until thick, stirring constantly. Add softened gelatin and stir until gelatin is dissolved. Chill until mixture begins to thicken. Gradually beat remaining sugar into stiffly-beaten egg whites. Add vanilla, then fold into slightly-thickened coffee-gelatin mixture. Turn into pie shell and chill until firm. Cover with whipped cream when ready to serve.

GRASSHOPPER PIE

30 marshmallows
1 cup milk
2 to 4 tablespoons crème de menthe, green-colored
1 ½ pints whipping cream
½ cup butter
1 package chocolate wafers, crushed

Melt marshmallows in milk over double boiler. Let cool. Add crème de menthe. Whip cream and fold into marshmallows. Melt butter and make pie crust by adding crushed wafers and molding into pie tin. Fill with marshmallow mixture and chill.

CHERRY CHIFFON PIE

1 envelope plain unflavored gelatin
¼ cup cold water
1 cup sugar
½ cup cherry juice from 1 can of sour pitted cherries, reserving cherries
  for topping
½ teaspoon salt
4 eggs, separated
½ teaspoon grated lemon rind
1 baked pie shell
½ pint whipping cream

Combine gelatin and cold water and let stand until thick. Combine ½ cup sugar, cherry juice, salt, and beaten egg yolks in the top of a double boiler. Cook over boiling water until thick and of a custard consistency. Add gelatin and lemon rind; cool until lukewarm. Beat egg whites with remaining 1/2 cup sugar until stiff. Fold into custard mixture. Fill pie shell and set in a cool place until firm. Top with whipped cream and cherries.

EGGNOG PIE

1 teaspoon unflavored gelatin
1 tablespoon cold water
1 cup milk
½ cup sugar
2 tablespoons cornstarch
¼ teaspoon salt
3 egg yolks, beaten
1 tablespoon butter
1 teaspoon vanilla
1 cup whipped cream
1 baked pie shell
Nutmeg

Soak gelatin in cold water. Combine milk, sugar, cornstarch, and salt and mix thoroughly. Put in top of double boiler and cook until thick and smooth. Cook 15 minutes longer, stirring constantly. Stir a small amount of this mixture into egg yolks, return to double boiler, and cook a few minutes longer. Add gelatin and butter and let cool. Add vanilla. Fold whipped cream into custard and pour into pie shell. Sprinkle top generously with nutmeg. Chill pie in refrigerator until ready to serve.

LEMON MERINGUE PIE

3 tablespoons cornstarch
1 cup plus 2 tablespoons sugar
Grated rind of 1 lemon
4 tablespoons lemon juice
1 tablespoon butter
3 eggs, separated
1 ½ cups boiling water
1 baked pie shell (9 inch)
6 tablespoons sugar

Combine cornstarch with sugar in top of double boiler. Add lemon rind, lemon juice, butter, and beaten egg yolks. Mix well, then add boiling water very slowly. Cook over hot water until thick. Cool. Pour into baked pie shell. Beat egg whites until almost stiff, then add sugar while continuing to beat until stiff. Arrange on pie to entirely cover filling and bake in a 300 degree oven for 30 minutes.

PUMPKIN PIE

Ever try making a fresh pumpkin pie? You can obtain your fresh pumpkin meat in this manner: Cut pumpkin in half and remove seeds and fibers. Place on a pan in a 350 degree oven, open sides down. When both halves have collapsed, remove from oven and lift off rind. Now you can start to make your crust.

1 can pumpkin (2 cups)
1 teaspoon salt
1 ½ teaspoons cinnamon
1 ½ teaspoons cloves
½ teaspoon allspice
1 teaspoon vanilla
3 eggs
2 cups half-and-half or milk
1 cup brown sugar
1 large unbaked pie shell
½ pint whipping cream
½ cup slivered almonds (optional)

Place pumpkin in electric mixer bowl along with salt, spices, and vanilla. Add eggs one at a time, blending well. Add half-and-half and brown sugar and mix thoroughly. Pour mixture into pie shell and bake at 425 degrees for 10 minutes. Reduce heat to 350 degrees and bake 35 to 45 minutes longer until pie is firm. Do not overbake. Top with whipped cream and almonds.

RHUBARB PIE

You can make a strawberry-rhubarb pie by using 1 ½ cups strawberries and 1 ½ cups rhubarb for the filling.

Enjoy the flavors of this pie with a Sebastiani Pinot Noir.

3 cups rhubarb
4 tablespoons flour
1 ½ cups sugar
2 egg yolks, well-beaten
Pastry for 2 pie crusts (see Pie Crust on page 237)
1 tablespoon butter

Cut rhubarb into ½ inch pieces. Sprinkle with flour, then add sugar, and egg yolks and mix well. Pour into lined pie plate and dot mixture with butter. Cover with top crust or pastry strips and bake at 425 degrees for 30 minutes. Reduce heat to 325 degrees and bake another 30 minutes.

SHERRY CREAM PIE

Shell:
1 ½ cups crushed chocolate wafer cookies
¼ pound (1 cube) butter, melted

Filling:
1 envelope unflavored gelatin
1 ¼ cups cold milk
3 eggs, separated
½ cup sugar
⅛ teaspoon salt
¼ teaspoon nutmeg
½ cup sherry
½ pint whipping cream
1 square grated sweet bakers chocolate

Crush cookies very fine. Mix with butter and pat firmly into a 10-inch glass pie plate to form a shell. Chill 1 hour.

Filling:
Soften gelatin in ¼ cup milk. Put egg yolks in top of a double boiler, beating slightly. Add sugar and remaining milk; stir well and cook for 10 minutes, or

recipe continued on next page

until mixture coats a spoon. Remove from stove. Add gelatin, salt, and nutmeg to custard and stir until gelatin is dissolved. Add sherry slowly (so it won't curdle), stirring constantly. Place in refrigerator to thicken. Beat egg whites stiff and whip cream. Fold beaten egg whites into whipped cream gently. Fill pie shell with chilled custard mixture and top with whipped cream-egg white mixture. Sprinkle top with chocolate. Chill for 8 hours.

STRAWBERRY PIE

1 cup crushed fresh strawberries
1 cup sugar
¼ teaspoon salt
1 tablespoon cornstarch
1 baked pie shell
¾ cup whole fresh strawberries
½ pint whipping cream

Mix crushed strawberries with sugar, salt, and cornstarch. Boil until transparent. Fill pie shell with fresh whole strawberries, washed, and hulled. Pour cooked strawberries over whole strawberries and chill. Top with whipped cream before serving.

MISCELLANEOUS

Enjoy with a glass of
Sebastiani Symphony.

BANANA FRITTERS

1 cup flour
1 teaspoon baking powder
½ teaspoon salt
½ to ¾ cup milk
1 egg, well-beaten
1 tablespoon rum (optional)
1 or 2 ripe bananas
Sugar

Sift flour, baking powder, and salt. Add milk, egg, and rum, if desired, and beat well. Skin and scrape the bananas; cut in half lengthwise, then across, making 4 pieces. Drop into batter and lift out with fork (do not pierce). Fry in hot deep fat and drain well when nicely browned. Sprinkle liberally with sugar.

BRANDY SAUCE

1 cup water
¾ cup sugar
¼ cup butter
½ teaspoon salt
1 teaspoon grated orange peel (optional)
1 tablespoon cornstarch, dissolved in 1 tablespoon cold water
2 tablespoons brandy

Mix all ingredients except brandy together and cook 5 to 10 minutes until mixture thickens. Add brandy, stir, and serve.

OVEN-ROASTED CHESTNUTS

2 pounds chestnuts
3 tablespoons cooking oil
3 tablespoons Sebastiani Cabernet Sauvignon, Zinfandel, or other dry,
   red wine

With a sharp knife, carefully cut a ½ inch gash on either side of the shells of chestnuts. Heat oil in a heavy skillet and add chestnuts. Shake over heat for 5 minutes. Roast in 450 degree oven for another 5 to 10 minutes. When cooked, cover chestnuts with a cloth that has been soaked in wine. Allow to stand 5 minutes and serve.

RAW CRANBERRY SAUCE

1 package cranberries
1 large orange, whole and unpeeled
2 apples, unpeeled
2 ½ cups sugar

Chop or grind cranberries. Remove seeds from orange and core apples. Grind orange, apples, and cranberries together, then add sugar. Put into covered jars and refrigerate. Sauce freezes extremely well.

HARD SAUCE

¼ cup butter
1 cup powdered sugar
1 teaspoon brandy

Cream butter, add sugar gradually, then add brandy. Use as a sauce over steamed puddings. If you prefer a thinner sauce, add more brandy.

PICKLED CUCUMBERS

Whole cucumbers, 3 to 5 inches long
1 stalk green dill
2 tablespoons mustard seed
4 red pickling chili peppers
6 cloves garlic
¼ teaspoon alum
4 tablespoons salt
1 part cold vinegar (about 2 ½ cups)
2 parts cold water (about 5 cups)

Pack cucumbers in a gallon jar. Place dill, mustard seed, peppers, garlic, alum, and salt in jar along with cucumbers. Boil vinegar with water; pour into jar and seal. Let stand 3 weeks.

BAKED MUSHROOMS

Serves 4–6

1 pound button mushrooms, sliced
½ teaspoon powdered oregano
¼ cup cracker meal
1 tablespoon lemon juice
4 tablespoons grated Parmesan cheese
1 clove garlic, minced
2 tablespoons olive oil
2 teaspoons chopped parsley
Salt, pepper to taste

Wash and drain mushrooms. Place in shallow baking dish. Combine oregano, cracker meal, lemon juice, cheese, garlic, and oil. Mix well, adding salt and pepper to taste. Sprinkle mixture over mushrooms. Bake 15 minutes at 350 degrees. Sprinkle with parsley before serving.

Accompany with a bottle of Sebastiani Zinfandel.

OYSTER OR ITALIAN MUSHROOMS

Serves 3–4

1 ½ cups mushrooms
3 tablespoons oil
2 tablespoons butter
1 clove garlic, chopped or pressed
¼ cup tomato sauce
¼ cup Sebastiani Chardonnay, or other dry, white wine
Grated Parmesan cheese

Cut mushrooms into pieces and boil about 20 minutes. Drain well. Sauté mushrooms in oil and butter in frying pan. Add garlic, tomato sauce, and wine. When mushrooms are cooked, add cheese as desired, stir once, and serve warm.

BAKED OYSTER MUSHROOMS

Mushrooms
Chopped parsley
Chopped garlic
Oregano
Bread crumbs
Olive oil
Salt, pepper to taste

Wash mushrooms thoroughly and drain well. Place in single layers on cookie sheet and sprinkle generously with remaining ingredients. Bake in top of oven at 350 degrees until moisture is absorbed. If browning is desired, place under broiler for a few minutes and watch carefully so that mushrooms do not burn.

The quantity of mushrooms in this recipe is optional. Use condiments to suit your taste.

STALE BREAD FRITTER

½ cup flour
½ cup milk
1 egg
1 teaspoon baking powder
½ teaspoon salt
5 slices stale bread, crusts removed
4 tablespoons sugar
1 teaspoon cinnamon

Mix flour, milk, egg, baking powder, and salt into a batter. Cut each slice of bread into 4 long pieces. Dip bread into batter and fry in hot deep fat; drain well. Sprinkle with sugar and cinnamon.

SPICED NUTS

Makes about 1 pound

2 ½ cups walnut halves
1 cup sugar
1 teaspoon salt
1 teaspoon cinnamon
⅓ cup milk
1 teaspoon vanilla

Spread walnuts in shallow pan and roast for 20 minutes at 275 degrees. Remove as soon as nuts are cool enough to handle. Rub between hands, removing as much brown skin as possible. In saucepan, combine sugar, salt, cinnamon, and milk. Heat, stirring until sugar is dissolved. Boil until a few drops form a ball in cold water. Remove from heat and stir in vanilla. Add cooled walnuts and stir gently until creamy. Turn out onto waxed paper and separate nuts.

SHERRIED WALNUTS

Makes about 4 cups

1 ¾ cups brown sugar, packed
¼ teaspoon salt
¼ cup dry sherry
2 tablespoons light corn syrup
3 cups walnut halves
Granulated sugar

Blend brown sugar, salt, sherry, and corn syrup. Stir in walnut halves, mixing until well-coated. Drop walnuts into granulated sugar and roll around until they have absorbed as much sugar as possible. Place on waxed paper to dry.

SUGARED NUTS

Makes about 1 pound

3 cups almonds or walnuts
1 cup sugar
2 tablespoons honey
¼ cup water

If you use almonds, blanch and toast them. It is not necessary to do this to the walnuts. Combine sugar, honey, and water in a saucepan and cook until a few drops form a ball in cold water. Add nuts and stir until creamy. Separate the nuts and allow to cool.

CANNED OLIVES

1 gallon water
¼ pound salt
1 gallon cured olives
Alum

For spiced olives, use same procedure except add 1 small pickling chili pepper, 1 teaspoon pickling spice, and 4 cloves garlic to each quart jar before sealing.

Bring water and salt to boil in a large pot. Drop in olives and bring to second boil. After boiling, put in hot sterile quart jars. Add a pinch of alum to each jar (this keeps olives crisp) and seal.

DRY OLIVES

Rock salt
Dark, fully-ripened olives

Place a layer of rock salt on the bottom of a wooden or cardboard container. Spread a layer of olives over this, then another layer of rock salt. Repeat until all olives have been used. Shake container each day. Olives are cured after 1 week. Remove olives from salt and put into jars. If you are not going to use olives within 2 months, place them under refrigeration. These olives go well with stews made of lamb, goat, or venison.

CURED GREEN OLIVES

1 gallon green olives (picked in autumn when olives first begin to get color
  and prior to first frost)
5 ounces lye
1 ½ pounds salt
Water

Place olives in stone crock. Do not use any metal container. Mix lye with 2 gallons water and pour over olives. Use caution when handling lye as it is very caustic. Let olives stand 18 hours in this solution. Then pour off lye water again exercising caution, and wash olives until water is clear. Cover olives with 2 gallons water and ½ pound salt. After 24 hours, drain olives again and cover with 2 gallons water and ½ pound salt. Soak another 24 hours and repeat procedure. At end of third day, pack olives in jars, covering with brine. Keep refrigerated and wash with clear water before serving.

SPICED PRUNES

2 cups prunes
1 cinnamon stick
3 slices lemon
⅓ cup Tawny Port
Water

Combine all ingredients and cover completely with water. Cover and bring to a boil, then let simmer for about 15 minutes. Remove from heat, allow to cool, and refrigerate. The longer the prunes soak the tastier they will be.

COOKED PRUNES

Cover prunes with boiling water, then cover with lid, and allow to cool. Let soak for 24 hours in the refrigerator. The longer the prunes soak, the more plump they will get.

BREAD STUFFING

Makes 4 cups

1 cup chopped onion
½ cup chopped celery
2 cloves garlic, chopped
¼ cup butter
6 cups dry bread cubes, ½ inch cubes
¾ teaspoon salt
Dash pepper
1 ½ teaspoons poultry seasoning
1 ⅔ cups water or bouillon
½ cup chopped parsley
½ cup grated Parmesan cheese

For duck or goose, add ½ cup raisins to stuffing mixture.

Sauté onion, celery, and garlic in butter and combine with remaining ingredients. More water or bouillon may be added if necessary. Stuff into bird or bake in a separate baking dish for 45 minutes at 325 degrees.

TOMATO SAUCE

2 tablespoon olive oil
½ cup finely chopped onion
2 cups solid pack tomatoes, chopped and reserve liquid
6 tablespoons tomato sauce
1 tablespoon fresh basil or 1 teaspoon dried basil
1 teaspoon sugar
½ teaspoon salt
¼ teaspoon pepper

Heat oil in a saucepan; add onions and cook over moderate heat 7 to 8 minutes, until they are soft but not brown. Add tomatoes with reserved liquid, tomato sauce, basil, sugar, salt, and pepper. Reduce heat to a low simmer, covering pan partially, and let cook 40 minutes, stirring occasionally. Season to taste.

CANNING OR PRESERVING ITALIAN MUSHROOMS (MORETTI)

Proceed with caution before using the following recipe for mushrooms. Mushrooms can be very dangerous. If you are not an expert in knowing your mushroom varieties, leave them alone.

Mushrooms, thoroughly washed and cut into pieces
1 part distilled vinegar to 2 parts water
1 or 2 cloves garlic
1 or 2 tablespoons mixed pickling spices
Dried oregano
Salt
1 or 2 red chili peppers
Olive oil

The amount of liquid used in this recipe depends on the amount of mushrooms. Use enough liquid to cover all mushrooms well. Bring liquid to boil with salt. Place garlic and spices into a piece of cloth and tie securely so that it can be easily removed before canning procedure. Add this cloth bag to boiling water, then add mushrooms, and let boil 1 hour. Drain well and spread out on Turkish towel for 24 hours. Put mushrooms into sterile pint jars, add 1 or 2 red chili peppers to each jar, and fill with olive oil.

Another method for preparing mushrooms is to boil them as above and place them into jars, adding the boiled liquid and any spices you prefer. Top with a little olive oil and seal as if you were canning fruit. The mushrooms, along with their liquid, can also be put into milk cartons and placed in the freezer.

PICKLED TOMATOES

Few carrots, sliced into ¾ inch rounds
Several celery stalks, sliced
Cauliflower
Small white onions, peeled
Green tomatoes or cherry tomatoes (three-fourths mature)

Follow same recipe as given for Pickled Cucumbers on page 250, but add carrots, celery, cauliflower, and onions to jars along with tomatoes.

WINE JELLY

Makes about 5–6 glasses

I recommend Sebastiani Chardonnay, Zinfandel, or Barbera for use in this recipe.

2 cups any dry Sebastiani wine, white or red
3 cups sugar
½ bottle fruit pectin
Paraffin

Put wine in top of double boiler. Add sugar and mix well. Place over rapidly boiling water and heat until wine is hot and sugar is dissolved, stirring constantly. Remove from water at once and stir in pectin. Pour quickly into glasses and cover with paraffin at once.

ZUCCHINI RELISH

2 quarts ground zucchini
4 medium white onions
1 large red bell pepper
Salted water

Vinegar Sauce:
1 ½ cups brown sugar
2 ½ cups white vinegar
1 teaspoon tumeric
¼ teaspoon powdered cloves
1 teaspoon mustard

Remove seeds and soft pulp from zucchini. Grind zucchini, onions, and bell pepper together. Place in a pot and cover with salted water. Let stand 4 hours then drain well. Make vinegar sauce by boiling all ingredients together until spices are dissolved. Put in drained zucchini, onions, and pepper and bring to a second boil, stirring well. Fill pint jars and seal.

WINE

WINE IN COOKING

As you will note in my recipes, I use a lot of wine in my cooking. It gives a flavor to certain dishes that cannot be obtained otherwise—many foods would be bland and flat without it. The flavor in wine is due to the nature of wine and not the alcohol. The alcohol escapes during cooking and none is present in the finished dish.

An all purpose wine for cooking is a good, sound, dry white wine—such as Chardonnay. The dry red wines are good, but they present a problem as they will darken certain dishes. They are compatible with dishes like stews, minestrone, and certain types of roast meats. I use and recommend a fresh bottle of wine for cooking, but a partially full bottle can be kept in the refrigerator for a week for cooking purposes.

Many of my friends use varying amounts of wine in recipes similar to mine— this is all a matter of experience and personal preference.

WINE IN OUR FAMILY

I grew up in a family where wine was part of our everyday living. It was just as much a part of mealtime as salt and pepper. A lunch or dinner without wine would not seem right. I recall that my father-in-law's dad, old Lorenzo, would absolutely refuse to sit down for his meals unless a bottle of wine was already on the table. If he did not have his glass of wine or two with his meal, we knew he was not well, which was not often as he lived to be 94. In spite of the presence of wine at all meals, temperance prevailed. Wine was always treated with respect as a part of our life. It was even given to the young—diluted with water.

If you went to visit one of the old-timers and he offered you some of his favorite wine, you would have insulted him if you had not at least taken a taste of it. During Prohibition most of the farmers that we knew made their own wines, and each one thought his wine was better than his neighbor's. They made wine with pride, treated it with care, and their wine cellars were a very important part of their homes. I recall one time when my husband bought a piece of farmland from an old Frenchman. Part of the consideration he had to make to his old friend was that he would furnish him with a gallon of wine per week for the balance of his life! On cold winter nights a visit to a friend's home would often bring out hot roasted chestnuts and a good bottle of red wine. Many were the Sunday afternoons I would see some of the men sit out under a tree in the backyard with an ice bucket and some good white wine, sipping the time away.

In my home, I have a large assortment of red and white wines, as well as sherries, ports, sparkling wines, and a few bottles of dry and sweet vermouth. With the exception of breakfast, wine is available with all meals. When I have company, I often serve wine in place of cocktails.

I have found that I get a great deal of satisfaction in knowing that I always have a few bottles of our special vintages or reserve selections put away for those extra special occasions. I am sure that you will find, too, that by having some of these special wines put away they will become the highlight of any meal.

I have enjoyed many different wines over the years with many combinations of meals, and there are no hard and fast rules, but the following is a guide to approaching wine and food pairing.

STORAGE

All wines with cork closures should be stored on their sides to ensure the cork stays moist. Air is the prime enemy of wine, and keeping the cork wet prohibits air's entry into the bottle. Fortified wines, such as port and sherry, are an exception to this rule; these wines may be stored with the neck up.

The temperature of storage should be as even as possible year around, and the ideal is from 50 to 55 degrees Fahrenheit. If you are going to use a binning cellar, a bin that permits selection of any bottle is usually the best, so that you don't have to disturb others to take one.

If at all possible, store your wines in the dark. Light, too, is an enemy of long-term storage, especially for wines bottled in clear glass.

GLASSWARE

Clear glassware shows the brilliant color of wine. The color of the wine in opaque or tinted glass is changed. Glassware should be as thin as possible and should be tulip-shaped with the upper rim turning inwards in order to direct the aroma and bouquet to your nose. Metal goblets should not be used for wine service, as they do not do justice to their contents. They do not allow observance of the true color of the wine and, in most cases, seem to give a metallic flavor to the wine.

A good all-purpose wine glass is a clear, stemmed 6- to 9-ounce capacity glass. You can use it to serve all wines, including sparkling and dessert wines. For table and sparkling wines, fill with about 5 ounces. For dessert and appetizer wines, fill with 2 to 3 ounces.

If you prefer, however, you can use 2 ½- to 4-ounce, tulip-shaped dessert wine glasses for both appetizer and dessert wines; tulip-shaped 9-ounce glasses for dinner wines; and champagne flutes for sparkling wines. The champagne glasses hold 5 ounces and can either be tulip or flute shaped.

TABLE SETTING

Wine glasses are usually placed at the right. If more than one wine is to be served, the glass for the first wine is placed the farthest to the right. If you are serving an elaborate meal, no more than three wine glasses should be in front of each guest at any time. Remove used glasses after each course is finished.

SERVING TEMPERATURES

The proper temperature for serving sparkling wine is about 40 degrees Fahrenheit. This temperature can be obtained by putting the sparking wine in a pail of cracked ice and water for 30 minutes or putting it in the coldest part of the refrigerator for about an hour. White still wines (non-sparkling), such as Chablis, Chenin Blanc, Chardonnay, Johannisberg Riesling, Gewürztraminer, and Sauvignon Blanc, should be at about 50 degrees Fahrenheit. This would be about 20 minutes in cracked ice and water or about 45 minutes in the refrigerator, and they may be served immediately after opening. Rosé wines should be treated and served as the white wines.

Still red wines, such as Pinot Noir, Merlot, Zinfandel, Barbera, and Cabernet Sauvignon, should be served at 65 to 70 degrees Fahrenheit (cellar temperature). Some reds are good cooler—Gamay and young, light reds can even be refrigerated a little before serving. Stand older bottles up for a couple of hours before serving. This will allow any sediment to settle to the bottom of the bottle. Remember, the correct temperature brings out the beauties of wines; incorrect temperatures hide the aromas and delicate flavors that you may expect. Do not replace the cork once the serving has begun. Naturally, it should be replaced when the wine is to be put away for a day or so of storage.

OPENING AND SERVING

The proper method of opening and serving wines would be as follows for sparkling wine: always hold the bottle so that it is pointed in a safe direction (away from anyone's face). Wipe the bottle dry, untwist the loop on the wire cage by bending from side to side, and then remove the wire cage and the top of the cap. Hold the cork firmly with the left hand (using a napkin if preferred) and twist the bottle—held at a 45 degree angle—with the right hand, holding it near the bottom of the bottle. When the cork turns in the bottle, continue to twist the bottle until you feel the cork rising. Then try to keep the cork from coming out too quickly. Ease it out, so as to let the gas escape gradually. During the whole operation, use great care to move the bottle gently, for agitating it releases the gas too quickly. Carefully wipe off the inside of the mouth of the bottle. When pouring, do not wrap the bottle in a napkin, but have one in the left hand under the bottle to catch either the sweat of the bottle or a drip that might fall on the tablecloth. As you finish pouring into a glass, twist the bottle as you bring the mouth of the bottle up to prevent dripping.

For all still wines, after the wine is brought to the proper temperature, cut off the top of the foil capsule ¼ inch or so down the neck of the bottle. Stand the bottle on a flat surface and hold it firmly. Insert the corkscrew in the middle of the cork. Screw it down straight, so that the end of the corkscrew will be at or below the bottom of the cork.

Pull slowly and carefully so as not to shake the bottle. I recommend a lever cork-screw as used by sommeliers in the better restaurants. Wipe the mouth of the bottle and pour with a napkin as for Champagne.

Many gourmet shops have wine coasters available in which your bottle may be placed while not in use. These are decorative on the table, as well as practical for keeping linen tablecloths clean. Bottle collars are also used to stop any drips from reaching the base of the bottle. These collars are also quite attractive and add to the conversation value of the wine when served.

WHAT WINES WITH WHAT FOODS

The heritage of wine and food dates back to the very beginning of civilization. In the Old Testament there is mention of Noah planting a vineyard. In King Tut's tomb, archeologists found wine jars. And the Romans and Greeks were known for their enjoyment of food and wine as early as 500 B.C. Our tradition of wine-making is based on our belief that wines are meant to be enjoyed with food. We believe careful thought should go into selecting wines for meals. One of our most frequently asked questions is: How does one select a good wine? Our answer is simple and dates back to my father-in-law who said "Quando un bicchiere di vino invita il secondo…il vino e` buono," which means, "When one glass of wine invites a second . . . the wine is good." Simple but true. When you are match-ing food and wine the same holds true. There are no concrete rules. Enjoy what pleases you.

Still, there are some simple guidelines that can help you as you experiment with different combinations. When pairing, you can either match textures, flavors, and weights or contrast them. Pay attention to how the dish is prepared as well. Delicately flavored entrées usually match up best with delicately-styled wines. Robust foods such as game, beef, and spicy sauces seem perfectly suited to robust and full-bodied wines. So experiment with different types of wines and food to taste the differences. I believe that you will find, as I have, that as you taste vari-ous wines you will find one, or maybe two wines, that you especially prefer. This then should be your rule: Drink what you like with whatever foods you prefer. For example, if you settle on a Chardonnay, as I have, you will find that it goes quite well with steaks. I would not recommend a red wine with oysters, but my husband often drank it with some preparations of fish and poultry, such as duck. He preferred the red wines to white and drank them almost exclusively.

Covering this subject is not easy, but these are my recommendations. Every food has a complementary drink, and the best combination brings out the full qualities and flavors of each. Before the meal a sparkling wine serves to stimulate appetites, relax any tensions of the day, and begin the evening with a connoisseur's touch. This also gives the cook time to let everyone arrive before putting on the last minute dishes.

I have drawn up a guide (below) of the wines Sebastiani produces and the food with which they are ideally suited. This will serve as a starting point for you, but when you find a wine you like, don't concern yourself with the rules—let your palate be the judge. If you enjoy it with a dish, drink it.

Red Wine Recommendations (in order of heartiness):

Cabernet Sauvignon	Cheeses (robust), Stews
Zinfandel	Steaks, Roasts, Chops
Merlot	Game
Barbera	Lamb, Duck
Pinot Noir	Casseroles, Spaghetti, Sausages

White Wine Recommendations:

Chardonnay	Poultry, Soups, Fish
Eye of the Swan	Fruits, Fruit Salads
Symphony	Cheeses (mild)

COMPARING WINES

At this point some notes on tasting and judging wines may be of interest. It is impossible to taste any beverage fairly if you have previously formed an opinion of it. Try to be as unprejudiced as possible. If you ask friends to pass judgment, do not let them know what they are tasting, and try to avoid imparting any hint of your opinion (good or bad). Before tasting, be sure that the wine in the glass is of the proper temperature, that you have the correct glass, and if there is any sediment, be sure it has settled to the bottom of the bottle. The glass should not be more than one-quarter full. Look for clarity, good color, and aromas and flavors that will give you pleasure to drink. Again, we believe that if one glass invites the second, the wine is good.

When tasting wine, one should use all of the senses. Hold your glass by the stem and observe the wine's color and appearance. Look first for clarity, a characteristic known to tasters as "candle-bright." Second, look for color. Is it correct for that type of wine? A dry white should be pale gold or yellow, not dark or browning. If it is a sparkling wine, judge for effervescence. The bubbles should be very small, consistently rising and breaking the surface. Then swirl your glass to vaporize the alcohol and increase the volatiles. Smell the wine and savor its bouquet and aroma. Put your nose over the middle of the glass and inhale deeply. It should smell clean with no corky or moldy smell, or doubtful aroma. The aroma should be completely harmonious. You should detect a delicate bouquet, and you should note the characteristics of that particular type of wine. Taste it, "trilling" to bring air into your mouth so as to cover the four groups of tasting glands on your tongue; this makes the flavors more apparent. Look first for cleanness, second for sweetness or acidity. Distinguish between acidity and sourness. Don't conclude it is sour if it is simply dry. Sourness means the presence of acetic acid—that unpleasant vinegary taste. Third, look for body. Is it thin and watery, or does it fill your mouth with flavor? Is the general impression pleasing? The answer to this question is most important. And then last, is it true to type? In every type there are decided differences in flavor, aromas, and other characteristics. You should not condemn a Chenin Blanc because it is not like a Chardonnay. They are both perfect types of wines in spite of their pronounced and different individualities. Slowly sip a small glass and note the finish as you swallow. The "aftertaste," or "finish," should be clean and pleasant and create the desire for another glass.

INDEX

POULTRY

GAME

SALADS

MISCELLANEOUS

WINE